Fairer, Faster And Firmer —
A Modern Approach to Immigration And Asylum

Presented to Parliament by the Secretary of State for the Home Department
by Command of Her Majesty.
July 1998.

Cm 4018

£8.65

Also available on the internet at
http://www.official-documents.co.uk/document/cm40/4018/4018.htm
or via http://www.homeoffice.gov.uk/index.htm

FAIRER, FASTER AND FIRMER —
A MODERN APPROACH TO IMMIGRATION AND ASYLUM

PREFACE

BY

THE HOME SECRETARY

Immigration control affects all of us in one way or another. When we travel abroad on holiday or business, we expect to be able to pass quickly through UK immigration control. Similarly, when our relatives or friends living abroad visit this country we expect them to be able to do so with a minimum of fuss. But we rightly expect our immigration controls to deal quickly and firmly with those who have no right to enter or remain here.

Piecemeal and ill-considered changes over the last 20 years have left our immigration control struggling to meet those expectations. Despite the dedication and professionalism of immigration staff at all levels, the system has become too complex and too slow, and huge backlogs have developed. Perversely, it is often the genuine applicants who have suffered, whilst abusive claimants and racketeers have profited. The cost to the taxpayer has been substantial and is increasing.

This White Paper sets out a comprehensive, integrated strategy to deliver a fairer, faster and firmer approach to immigration control as we promised in our manifesto. Fundamental to the whole strategy is the need to modernise procedures and deliver faster decisions. The Government believes that there are too many avenues of appeal in the course of a single case. There should be a single appeal right considering the case as a whole, including removal arrangements. We must also regulate unscrupulous advisers who exploit the vulnerable and profit from delays.

We must be able to plan and allocate resources more flexibly in order to minimise costs overall. In particular, that means investing to eliminate backlogs and produce a fairer and faster system – and increased effort to enforce immigration controls so that those who are refused understand that they must go.

The UK was one of the first countries to sign up to the 1951 Geneva Convention on Refugees, designed in the aftermath of the last war to ensure the humane treatment of those who had to flee their own country because of a well-founded fear of persecution. But the Convention never anticipated the dramatic changes in the speed, relatively low cost and easy availability of international travel and telecommunications. In recent years our asylum system has been under severe strain. The numbers of people claiming asylum has increased from about 4,000 a year in 1988 to over 32,000 in 1997. The Government is committed to protecting genuine refugees. Indeed, it is plainly absurd for those who have fled persecution from abroad to have to wait months, or even years, to hear they are allowed to stay. But there is no doubt that large numbers of economic migrants are abusing the system by claiming asylum. Modernising our controls and simplifying our procedures will help to tackle that problem.

The current arrangements for supporting asylum seekers are a shambles. New arrangements are needed to ensure that genuine asylum seekers are not left destitute, but which minimise the attractions of the UK to economic migrants. Those arrangements and our overhaul of the asylum system are based on recognising and fulfilling the mutual obligations – a new covenant – that exist between the Government and those seeking asylum here.

The Government's approach to immigration control reflects our wider commitment to fairness. We have moved further and faster than any of our predecessors in buttressing the rights of people in relation to public authorities. The Human Rights Bill currently going through Parliament will prove a

landmark in the development of a fair and reasonable relationship between individuals and the state in this country. This is an important backdrop to the proposals in this White Paper.

The White Paper sets out a long-term strategy. It tackles the failings of the current system and addresses the challenges which face our immigration control in the years ahead. It fulfils our commitment to develop a fairer, faster and firmer approach in the interests of all our people.

JACK STRAW
July 1998

SUMMARY OF PROPOSALS

1. The fair and efficient control of immigration is one of the most important tasks for any Government. In one way or another, the operation of immigration control affects every citizen of this country. A modern immigration control must recognise the extent of international travel and seek to facilitate legitimate travellers as well as preventing people entering or remaining in the country if they have no right to do so. International travel is of enormous economic and social benefit to this country and reflects the UK's position within the European Union (EU).

2. In the light of the Comprehensive Spending Review process, the Government intends to modernise the whole approach to immigration in order to improve the quality of service to UK citizens and those who qualify to enter or remain here, as well as to strengthen the necessary controls on those who do not. This White Paper sets out the Government's comprehensive strategy for modernising our immigration control. The key features of the strategy are that the future operation of immigration control will be:

- integrated in order to maximise efficiency and minimise the scope for abuse;

- informed and more open; and

- fairer, faster and firmer.

3. An informed approach to immigration control must be based on a clear understanding of current immigration trends. Chapter 1 summarises those trends, while the Government's broad policy objectives, including retention of frontier controls and the commitment to promoting race equality, are set out in Chapter 2. The Government is also determined that the new strategy should remedy the failings of the current system (Chapter 3), in particular:

- delays and backlogs which increase costs and undermine the integrity of the control;

- outdated and complex procedures which hinder genuine travellers and are vulnerable to abuse; and

- a piecemeal approach which has failed to tackle the underlying problems.

4. The Government believes that an integrated approach to modernisation and streamlining of the control provides the way ahead (Chapter 4). The subsequent chapters of the White Paper examine the constituent parts of the control from pre-entry through to settlement and citizenship or, on the other hand, removal of those with no right to be here.

An integrated approach

5. The key to modernising and streamlining the control is to see the system as a whole. In that way, the control can be operated more effectively to speed the passage of genuine travellers and to target resources on those seeking to evade the control. The Government will:

- establish a single management structure in the UK to manage the entry clearance operation overseas, and to provide more effective links with the on-entry and after-entry controls (paragraph 5.6);

- maximise the use of modern technology to integrate the pre-entry, on-entry and after-entry systems to help speed passenger clearance and target evasion of the control (paragraphs 6.10–6.11);

- integrate the use of intelligence throughout the system in order to target resources more effectively and improve multi-agency co-operation to tackle abuse and racketeering (paragraph 6.12);

- modernise the immigration, asylum and nationality casework processes by introducing a new computerised and integrated casework system (paragraphs 7.2-7.5);

- create a new inter-departmental planning and monitoring process to enable resources to be used more effectively, particularly by bringing most funding for support of asylum seekers into a single budget managed by the Home Office (paragraphs 8.22 and 13.7).

An informed and more open approach

6.   The Government is committed to greater openness in relation to immigration control as in other areas of public life. Greater openness helps to ensure that decisions about changes to the control are better informed and sustains public confidence in the integrity of the control. It is also consistent with the Government's commitment to race equality, and to the principles set out in the Human Rights Bill. The Government has already taken steps to:

- ensure that reasons for refusal of British citizenship are always given (paragraphs 7.7 and 10.6);

- promote greater dialogue with those to whom the controls apply and representative interest groups by the development of user panels (paragraphs 7.8-7.9);

- develop a charter of rights and responsibilities for those coming into contact with the Immigration and Nationality Directorate (paragraph 7.10);

- publish the Immigration Directorates' Instructions and Asylum Directorate's Instructions so that users know the basis on which decisions affecting them will be made (paragraph 7.11).

Fairer, faster and firmer

7.   The fundamental objective of the Government's strategy is to deliver a modern control which is fairer, faster and firmer. Many of the measures described in this White Paper satisfy at least two of those requirements; some satisfy all three. The Government intends to introduce the following integrated package of measures to reform all stages of the control:

Pre, on and after-entry controls

- introduce a streamlined right of appeal for those refused a visa to visit a family member (paragraphs 5.7-5.10);

- take statutory powers to enable a pilot scheme to be run to test the merits of introducing a financial bond scheme for visitors to the UK (paragraphs 5.11-5.12);

- examine measures to ensure fuller compliance with the Immigration (Carriers' Liability) Act 1987 (paragraphs 5.13-5.14).

- invest immediately to increase the number of Airline Liaison Officers to help reduce the number of inadequately documented passengers coming to the UK (paragraphs 5.18-5.20);

- modernise the framework of immigration law to enable the controls to be exercised more flexibly to speed the passage of genuine travellers and target resources on potential abuse (paragraphs 6.6-6.9);

- take further measures to avoid racial discrimination by employers when making checks to prevent illegal working (paragraph 7.12(iv));

- develop new criteria to enable compassionate factors to be given due weight at every stage of the caseworking process (paragraph 7.12(v)).

Appeals

- speed up the process by a radical overhaul of the system of immigration and asylum appeals, reducing the number of avenues of appeal and reforming the structure of the Immigration Appellate Authority (paragraphs 7.13-7.18);

- consult those involved in the appeals process on how to make it more efficient (paragraph 7.19);

- statutory control of unscrupulous immigration advisers who exploit individuals and undermine the control (paragraphs 7.20-7.22);

- action to bring the use of legal aid under tighter control (paragraphs 7.23-7.27).

Asylum

- recognise the obligations of both the Government *and* asylum applicants – a new covenant (paragraph 8.5);

- faster decisions on asylum applications and appeals, including standardising the period allowed post-interview for the submission of further material before decision (paragraphs 8.7-8.9 and 8.11);

- create new support arrangements to ensure that asylum seekers are not left destitute, minimise the incentive to economic migration, remove access to Social Security benefits, minimise cash payments and reduce the burden on local authorities (paragraphs 8.12-8.26);

- no amnesty but adopt measures, including additional resources, to tackle the backlogs inherited from the previous Government (paragraphs 8.27-8.32);

- abolish the qualifying period for grant of settlement to those given refugee status and reduce it for those granted exceptional leave to remain (paragraph 9.3);

- develop arrangements to provide high quality information about countries of origin which are more systematic and more transparent (paragraphs 9.4-9.6);

- introduce new guidelines to help ensure that the claims of those in genuine need of protection are identified quickly (paragraph 9.7);

- the separate procedure for certain listed countries (the "White List") will be abolished, but manifestly unfounded cases will continue to be put into an accelerated appeal procedure, whatever their country of origin (paragraphs 9.9-9.10).

Citizenship

- take effective action to reduce waiting times for dealing with applications for British citizenship (paragraphs 10.3-10.5);

- create a more flexible approach to the residence requirements in the British Nationality Act 1981 (paragraph 10.7).

Enforcement

- strengthen existing criminal offences to enable more effective prosecution of applications involving blatant deceit (paragraph 11.3);

- tackle the problem of bogus marriages by enhancing the powers of registrars (paragraphs 11.4-11.5);

- develop a more proactive, intelligence led and multi-agency approach to combat immigration-related crime (paragraphs 11.6-11.8);

- extend the powers of immigration officers to enable more enforcement operations to be conducted without having to rely on a police presence, and work to make the prosecution process for immigration offences more effective (paragraphs 11.9-11.12);

- examine the options for increased use of fingerprinting, and enhance the arrangements for securing documentation to strengthen the enforcement effort (paragraphs 11.14-11.18);

- evaluate the potential for increasing the number of passengers returned by use of readmission agreements and voluntary return programmes (paragraphs 11.19-11.23);

- pursue options to enable asylum seekers whose claims are properly the responsibility of other EU Member States to be transferred more quickly (paragraphs 11.24-11.30);

- support the conclusion of work on the Eurodac Convention to establish a computerised central database of fingerprints of asylum seekers and certain illegal immigrants across the EU (paragraphs 11.31–11.32).

Detention

- give written reasons for detention at the outset of all cases and thereafter at monthly intervals, or at shorter intervals in the case of detained families (paragraph 12.7);

- introduce a more extensive judicial element into the detention process in immigration and asylum cases (paragraphs 12.8–12.10);

- consider the need for an increase in the detention estate in order to support an increased number of removals (paragraphs 12.12–12.14);

- establish clear statutory rules covering all aspects of the management and administration of detention centres and be more open in future about private sector contracts in this area (paragraphs 12.15–12.18);

- seek specific powers for detention custody officers similar to those provided for prisoner custody officers (paragraph 12.19).

Implementation

8. Implementation of the strategy (Chapter 13) will require a major programme of work, including additional investment to strengthen the controls and reduce decision times. The Government is also introducing new budgeting and planning arrangements to make more effective use of resources. There will be a new single budget for asylum seeker support costs which will be managed by the Home Office. This will enable more flexible use of resources to reduce costs overall. There will also be a new integrated, inter-departmental planning process to manage the system as a whole more effectively. The Government will also explore whether a greater proportion of the costs of immigration control should be borne by users, including passengers, carriers and port authorities, rather than the taxpayer generally.

9. Implementation of some elements of the strategy will require changes in the law. The Government will introduce legislation for this purpose as soon as possible.

CONSULTATION

The Government invites views on the proposals in the Home Office and Lord Chancellor's Department Joint Consultation Paper on "Review of Appeals" (see paragraph 7.13). Copies of that document may be obtained from:

Justin Blackall
Asylum and Appeals Policy Directorate
Immigration and Nationality Directorate
7th Floor
Whitgift Centre – Block A
15 Wellesley Road
CROYDON
CR9 3LY

Written comments on the proposals should be sent to the following address by **12 October 1998:**

Kim Head
Asylum and Appeals Policy Directorate
Immigration and Nationality Directorate
7th Floor
Whitgift Centre – Block A
15 Wellesley Road
CROYDON
CR9 3LY

Any written comments on the proposals in this White Paper should be sent by **30 October 1998** to:

Liz McCarty
Strategy and Legislation Team
Immigration and Nationality Directorate
6th Floor
Whitgift Centre – Block A
15 Wellesley Road
CROYDON
CR9 3LY

The Government may be asked to publish responses to this White Paper. Please let us know if you do not want your comments to be published.

CHAPTER 1
CURRENT IMMIGRATION TRENDS

1.1 The contributions made by those who immigrated to Britain and their descendants are incredibly diverse. This year sees the 50th anniversary of the arrival of the SS Windrush at Tilbury Docks on 22 June 1948. The 492 passengers and all those who followed them have made an enormous contribution to today's British society. Every area of British life has been enriched by their presence. In politics and public life; the economy and public service; medicine, law, and teaching; and the cultural and sporting elements of our national life, individuals and communities have made a positive impact, helping Britain to develop. Part of that development is in our national identity, which now reflects our multi-cultural and multi-racial society.

Recent immigration trends

1.2 Over the last five years there has been little increase in the underlying trend of settlement by spouses and dependants coming to form or join families already here, or for employment purposes. In 1997, there were 43,000 acceptances for settlement in these categories out of total acceptances for settlement of 59,000. There will be a rise in the number of spouses accepted for settlement in 1998 as a result of the abolition of the primary purpose rule, but otherwise the long-term settlement trend is unlikely to rise significantly, apart from settlement following the grant of asylum and exceptional leave to remain (ELR).

Economic migration

1.3 Patterns of international migration are now much more complex. The UK, along with the rest of Western Europe, the USA, Canada and Australia has seen a substantial increase in the number of economic migrants seeking a better life for themselves and their families. There is, of course, nothing new about individuals travelling within and across international borders to improve their economic circumstances. This has been a permanent feature of human history. But modern communications and modern travel have been significant factors in changing the nature and extent of economic migration, facilitating the genuine traveller but also creating opportunities for those who seek to evade immigration control.

1.4 The availability of rapid, mass communication means much better access to information about the opportunities and economic circumstances in other parts of the world. People living in countries with weaker economies receive daily images of the potential economic and other social benefits available in richer countries across the globe. The knowledge of such opportunities, as it has always done, provides an incentive to economic migration, but it is now available to a much larger population. And that population is better informed about the comparative benefits of different countries, whether it be in relation to the nature of job opportunities, or other factors such as distance, ease of entry, welfare facilities, family ties, chances of being removed and language and cultural or historical links. The desire to move is obviously strengthened where relative poverty is combined with political instability.

Increase in travel

1.5 In recent years, the number of passengers travelling to the UK, including British citizens returning, has increased by an average of nearly 8% each year. Over the past five years, arrivals rose from 55 million in

Figure A

PASSENGER ARRIVALS[1] IN THE UNITED KINGDOM
(in millions)

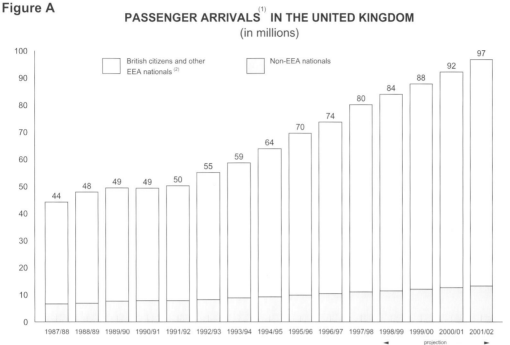

☐ British citizens and other EEA nationals [2]   ☐ Non-EEA nationals

Year	Value
1987/88	44
1988/89	48
1989/90	49
1990/91	49
1991/92	50
1992/93	55
1993/94	59
1994/95	64
1995/96	70
1996/97	74
1997/98	80
1998/99	84
1999/00	88
2000/01	92
2001/02	97

projection

(1) Including passengers of all nationalities in direct transit who did not pass through immigration control.
(2) Data for all years cover countries now in the European Economic Area.

1992/93 to 80 million in 1997/98 (see Figure A).

1.6   Most of this increase in travel stems from more people travelling abroad for legitimate purposes including business, study and holidays. As such, the growth in the number of passengers travelling to the UK is something which the Government welcomes and wishes to encourage. But access to cheap international travel has also provided a practical means by which economic migrants can seek to realise their desire for a better life. Rather than being confined to neighbouring countries within reach by more traditional forms of travel, economic migrants have a much wider range of choice about their country of destination.

1.7   The pressure to migrate results in individuals and groups seeking to enter the UK and other countries by whatever means available. They cannot normally satisfy the requirements of the Immigration Rules. They may seek to gain entry illegally or by claiming a status under the Immigration Rules to which they are not entitled. For this reason, it is necessary to view the immigration system as a whole, recognising that economic migrants will exploit whatever route offers the best chance of entering or remaining within the UK. That might mean use of fraudulent documentation, entering into a sham marriage or, particularly in recent years, abuse of the asylum process.

Growth in asylum claims

1.8   The UK is a signatory to the 1951 UN Convention Relating to the Status of Refugees and its 1967 Protocol. These require us to offer refuge to a person who:

> "owing to a well-founded fear of being persecuted for reasons of race, religion, nationality, membership of a particular social group or political opinion, is outside the country of his nationality and is unable or, owing to such fear, is unwilling to avail himself of the protection of that country; or who, not having a nationality and being outside the country of his former habitual residence

as a result of such events, is unable or, owing to such fear, is unwilling to return to it."

The Convention also requires signatories to make social welfare available to those recognised as refugees on the same basis as to its own citizens. The Government's aim is to create an efficient asylum system that helps genuine asylum seekers and deters abusive claimants.

1.9 For almost 40 years only small numbers of people, predominantly those fleeing communism, applied for asylum in the UK. Then, in the late 1980s the total started to rise dramatically from around 4,000 a year during 1985-1988 to 44,800 in 1991. Following the introduction of measures in November 1991 to deter multiple and other fraudulent applications, numbers fell back in 1992 and 1993. However, applications increased substantially in 1994 and again in 1995 (to

44,000), but, after falling back in 1996 (following the reduction in benefit entitlement for asylum seekers), continued rising in 1997 and early 1998 (see Figure B).

International comparisons

1.10 Many other western countries have also seen increases in the number of asylum seekers. Germany receives by far the most (136,000 in 1997), followed by the UK (41,500), Netherlands (34,000), Switzerland (24,000) and France (24,000) — figures including dependants. The number applying to most European countries seems to be rising, except in Germany where there have been large reductions reflecting changes in Eastern Europe and in Germany's immigration control. The distribution of asylum seekers between countries does vary in response to a wide range of factors in both source and destination countries. In the late 1980s other countries received much larger numbers than the UK (see Figure C).

Figure B

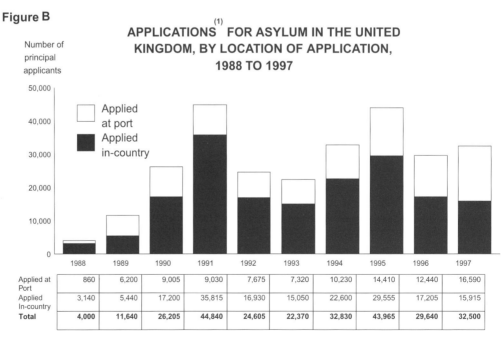

APPLICATIONS⁽¹⁾ FOR ASYLUM IN THE UNITED KINGDOM, BY LOCATION OF APPLICATION, 1988 TO 1997

Number of principal applicants

	1988	1989	1990	1991	1992	1993	1994	1995	1996	1997
Applied at Port	860	6,200	9,005	9,030	7,675	7,320	10,230	14,410	12,440	16,590
Applied In-country	3,140	5,440	17,200	35,815	16,930	15,050	22,600	29,555	17,205	15,915
Total	**4,000**	**11,640**	**26,205**	**44,840**	**24,605**	**22,370**	**32,830**	**43,965**	**29,640**	**32,500**

(1) Excluding dependants.

Figure C

Applications received for asylum in Europe, including dependants, by year of application, 1987 to 1997

	1987	1988	1989	1990	1991	1992	1993	1994	1995	1996	1997
Austria	11,400	15,800	21,900	22,800	27,300	16,200	4,400	N/A	N/A	N/A	N/A
Belgium	6,000	5,100	8,100	13,000	15,200	17,800	26,900	14,300	11,400	12,200	11,600
Denmark	2,800	4,700	4,600	5,300	4,600	13,900	14,400	6,700	5,100	5,900	5,100
Finland	50	50	200	2,500	2,100	3,600	2,000	800	900	700	1,000
France[1]	27,300	34,800	66,000	61,600	51,200	31,800	29,300	28,600	24,200	20,600	24,000
Germany[1]	74,600	134,000	157,300	250,900	332,800	569,600	419,400	165,400	166,300	151,300	135,700
Italy	11,000	1,300	2,200	4,700	31,700	2,600	1,600	1,800	1,800	600	1,700
Netherlands	13,500	7,500	14,000	21,200	21,600	20,300	35,400	52,600	29,300	22,900	34,400
Norway	8,600	6,600	4,400	4,000	4,600	5,200	12,900	3,400	1,500	1,800	2,300
Spain[1]	3,300	4,300	5,200	11,200	10,500	15,200	16,400	13,300	7,400	6,100	6,400[2]
Sweden	18,100	19,600	32,000	29,000	27,300	84,000	37,600	18,600	9,000	5,800	9,600
Switzerland	10,900	16,700	24,500	36,000	41,600	18,000	24,700	16,100	17,000	18,100	23,900
United Kingdom	5,900	5,700	16,800	38,200	73,400	32,300	28,000	42,200	55,000	37,000	41,500
Total	193,400	256,100	357,200	500,400	643,900	830,500	652,900	363,900	328,000	283,000	297,200

(1) Figures based on IGC data but adjusted to include an estimated number of dependants.

(2) Includes estimated figures for October to December 1997.

Who applies for asylum?

1.11   The majority of principal asylum applicants in the UK are relatively young: approximately two thirds are between 21 and 34 years old, with fewer than 5% aged 50 or older. In 1997, 87% of asylum applicants had no dependants at the time of application and about 75% of principal applicants were male. It is also significant that asylum seekers in the UK come from a wide spread of source countries (see Figure D).

1.12   This spread changes year by year in response to economic and political changes in countries across the world, although Somalia, Sri Lanka and Turkey have featured regularly over the last ten years. The make up of asylum applications has changed. Ten years ago applications were concentrated in a relatively small number of nationalities. There were either a lot of applications from a particular nationality or very few. Now there is a much more even spread of nationalities.

Who is granted asylum?

1.13   In 1997, 36,000 initial decisions were made on asylum applications. Of those, 4,000 (over 10%) were to recognise the applicant as a refugee and grant asylum. Nearly half of those cases were nationals of the former Yugoslavia (mostly Bosnians) and 25% were Somalis. In addition, 3,100 (9%) of total initial decisions were not to recognise as a refugee, but to grant ELR because of genuine humanitarian factors. Somalis accounted for over 30% of that category, Afghans nearly 20% and former Yugoslavs over 10%.

Abuse of the asylum system

1.14   There is no doubt that the asylum system is being abused by those seeking to migrate for purely economic reasons. Many claims are simply a tissue of lies. Some of these are made on advice from unscrupulous "advisers" simply as a means of evading control or prolonging a stay in the UK

Figure D

Number of
principal
applicants

TOP TWELVE NATIONALITIES [1] CLAIMING ASYLUM IN THE UNITED KINGDOM 1997

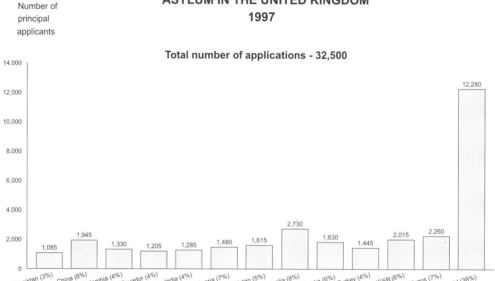

Total number of applications - 32,500

(1) Excluding dependants

without good reasons. Around three-quarters of asylum applications are refused because they do not meet the requirements for refugee status or ELR. The vast majority of such failed applicants appeal, but only 6% of those appeals are successful. The abuse of the system demonstrated by these figures is also illustrated in the following examples:

Case study: the applicant arrived at Heathrow in April 1997 and claimed asylum. His application was refused in May 1997. He made a series of further representations, including taking legal proceedings to obtain payment of income support. In those proceedings, he conceded that the account which he gave when seeking asylum was a series of lies. The proceedings for payment of income support also failed.

Case study: the applicant first arrived in the UK in April 1998 with his wife, and they were granted entry as visitors. He was later arrested by immigration officers for working unlawfully, and was treated as an illegal entrant. He subsequently claimed asylum, and was granted temporary release. A few days later he was arrested for the same offence. At this time he withdrew his asylum claim and was removed to Lithuania.

He flew back to the UK four days later and sought leave to enter for two to three weeks, claiming he wanted to collect some cars he had bought when he was last in the UK. Having denied having any problems previously, he was refused leave to enter as a visitor and immediately claimed asylum. His asylum application has now been refused.

> *Case study:* the applicant sought
> entry for three weeks to visit her
> brother. Following refusal,
> representations were received
> seeking a visit for six months for the
> same purpose. When that application
> was also refused, an asylum claim
> was lodged by legal representatives
> who said the applicant had a well-
> founded fear of persecution if
> returned to Malawi. That application
> was refused and the passenger
> detained. Upon detention, the asylum
> claim was formally withdrawn and
> the applicant asked to return home as
> soon as possible. Within 24 hours,
> and while the return was being
> arranged, a renewed asylum claim
> was made.

The scale of illegal immigration

1.15   The very nature of illegal immigration makes it difficult accurately to assess the total number of people in the country without authority and so liable to removal. Excluding those with unresolved asylum claims or outstanding appeals, the Immigration Service is at present dealing with a total of about 20,000 enforcement cases and over 9,000 port cases of people liable for removal. These figures are likely to grow as greater efficiency elsewhere in the system means that the number of such cases continues to exceed our present ability to effect removals.

1.16   During 1997 some 6,500 persons were removed or departed voluntarily from the UK following enforcement action, of which around 3,000 were failed asylum seekers. The total number of removals and voluntary departures of failed asylum seekers, under port or enforcement procedures, has increased steadily over recent years from 1,800 in 1993 to 7,000 in 1997. The Government intends to pursue a range of measures to increase that number still further.

Growth in immigration racketeering

1.17   Illegal immigration is increasingly facilitated by organised criminals who use similar support structures and routes as drug traffickers. The International Organisation for Migration (IOM) estimated in 1996 that human trafficking was worth US$7 billion globally. It has also been estimated that at any one time about one million people are in the process of moving to western countries as part of organised trafficking. The causes of human trafficking – economic deprivation, over-population and social and political instability – are unlikely to be resolved in the short term.

Clandestine entry

1.18   Racketeering takes many forms, including clandestine entry, use of false documents, marriage abuse, and fraudulent asylum claims. The introduction of carriers' liability legislation and greater vigilance by airline staff at ports of embarkation has seen a resurgence in clandestine traffic, largely moribund throughout the 1980s. Immigrants are often obliged to work for their facilitators after entry in order to pay off their journey costs, in employment where pay and conditions are very poor and where their reluctance to complain is ruthlessly exploited. Others with no legitimate sources of income resort to crime to survive. It is difficult to estimate the true scale of the problem, but in 1997 there were over 4,000 known incidents of clandestine entry compared with under 500 in 1992. This method of evading the immigration control is continuing to increase, with over 2,700 known cases in the first five months of 1998.

Forged documentation

1.19   Other forms of racketeering are also on the increase. Unscrupulous legal representatives provide legal services and coaching for fraudulent asylum claims, "fixers" arrange marriages of convenience, some immigration advisers use fraud and deception to obtain legal residence for their clients. Criminal groups are realising that illegal entrants with no recourse to the authorities are fair game for exploitation in other ways, such as prostitution. Entry is often facilitated by means of fraudulently obtained documents or increasingly sophisticated forgeries. In 1997 around 4,500 suspect travel documents were detected, over 70% of which were European Economic Area documents. This represents a 26% increase on 1996 figures, with current figures suggesting a further rise to a total in excess of 6,000 in 1998.

Expected future trends

1.20   The pressures on our immigration control are likely to continue to increase and will change in nature. For example, the number of people who are subject to immigration control will change as additional candidate countries join the EU and their citizens then benefit from rights of free movement under European Community law. The growth in passenger arrivals over the next few years is projected to average about 5% a year, increasing the number of arrivals to about 97 million by 2001/02. As at present, the vast majority of these passengers will be legitimate travellers. It will be vital to our business and other interests that they should be admitted quickly. But, unless action is taken, that growth in traffic will also bring a substantial increase in the number of inadequately documented or otherwise inadmissible passengers with whom our immigration control must also be able to deal quickly and firmly.

1.21   The current trend in respect of asylum applications (excluding dependants) in the UK suggests further increases to nearly 38,000 in 1998/99 and to 44,000 in 1999/00. At that rate, there would be about 50,000 applications in 2000/01. It is asylum applications which will have the greatest impact on the settlement figures in the coming years.

CHAPTER 2

POLICY PRINCIPLES

2.1 Any strategy for immigration control must, as well as reflecting operational requirements, satisfy fundamental policy principles. Chief among these are respect for human rights and for race equality.

Fair, fast and firm

2.2 Every country must exercise firm control over immigration and Britain is no exception. This Government will not allow our controls to be abused with impunity and will ensure that the controls are modernised and that the staff who operate them are equipped to carry out their tasks effectively. But we shall also ensure that controls are operated speedily and fairly. The vast majority of passengers arriving at our ports or applying to remain here have legitimate reasons for doing so. The control must operate in a way which provides them with a fast and efficient service and so helps to promote travel and business which contribute substantially to our economy. All staff applying the Government's immigration and nationality policy will observe these central principles of being fair, fast and firm; and will carry out their duties without regard to the race, colour or religion of any person seeking to enter or remain in the UK, or applying for citizenship. The Government believes that greater openness has a key role in a fair, fast and firm immigration control.

Key objectives

2.3 In furtherance of these broad statements of policy, the key objectives of the Government's policy on immigration and nationality are to:

- welcome genuine visitors and students who wish to come to the UK;

- support family life by admitting the spouses and minor dependent children of those already settled in the UK;

- ensure that asylum decisions are both swift and fair and fully meet the UK's obligations towards refugees under international law;

- grant entry to those who qualify for periods of work in the UK;

- maintain a fair, fast and effective entry clearance operation at UK posts overseas;

- give effect to the "free movement" provisions of European Community law while retaining controls at frontiers, operated by a civilian Immigration Service;

- detect and remove those entering or remaining in the UK without authority and take firm action against those profiting from abuse of the immigration laws, including effective preventative measures; and

- grant applications for citizenship to those meeting the specified criteria.

Human rights

2.4 Legislation is currently before Parliament to allow people access to their rights under the 1950 European Convention on Human Rights (ECHR) in our domestic courts. The Human Rights Bill makes it unlawful for public authorities to act in a way which is incompatible with the Convention rights. That will apply, for example, to decisions of immigration officers, special adjudicators, and the Secretary of State. The Government has given a commitment that an order-making power in the Human Rights Bill will be used to enable an asylum seeker whose application has been refused to appeal also on the grounds that his removal from the UK would breach ECHR rights.

2.5 Once the Bill becomes law it will be a major defence against arbitrary or unreasonable behaviour by public authorities. This will ensure that measures to make our controls firmer and faster do not compromise on fairness. The Government sees its commitment to strengthen human rights as going hand in hand with the proposals in this White Paper.

European and international context

2.6 By its very nature, immigration control has to function in an international context. We subscribe to various sets of international rules which govern our actions and also benefit from international co-operation – in sharing intelligence, in mounting joint operations and in developing joint policies – which is essential if we are to tackle trafficking which is itself organised on an international scale.

International obligations

2.7 One of the principal international conventions of relevance in this field is the 1951 UN Convention Relating to the Status of Refugees. This was signed with all-party support and the UK's obligations arising under it have been scrupulously observed by successive governments. The Government works closely with UN officials in seeking to make the Convention work in a fair and sensible way. The Government is also committed to implement European Community (EC) provisions on free movement for EC nationals and their dependants. At the same time the Government will continue to ensure that those rights, particularly as they concern third country national family members, are not abused.

International co-operation

2.8 Traffickers operate across all continents. No prosperous western country is immune from being targeted. Complex routes involving a mix of countries can be followed to evade controls. Profits and payments are likewise distributed on an international scale. It is essential if law enforcement agencies are

to control this activity that they too must work internationally and the Government is strongly committed to developing such co-operation. We were the first country to ratify the Europol Convention and supported the decision to give Europol a role in combatting illegal immigration. The Government has played an active part in work to develop the Eurodac Convention to create a computerised central database of fingerprints of asylum seekers across the EU and supported its extension to certain illegal migrants. We shall continue to strengthen co-operation of this kind.

Retaining frontier controls

2.9 The main focus of UK immigration control has traditionally been at the point of entry. For the UK, frontier controls are an effective means of controlling immigration, and of combatting terrorism and other crime. These controls match both the geography and traditions of the country and have ensured a high degree of personal freedom within the UK. This approach is different from the practice in mainland Europe where, because of the difficulty of policing long land frontiers, there is much greater dependence on internal controls such as identity checks. We need to recognise these differences.

2.10 The Government has already made clear its commitment to maintaining the UK system of frontier controls and we have translated that commitment into practice. In the negotiations last year in the Inter-Governmental Conference which culminated in the Treaty of Amsterdam, the Government sought and obtained legally binding confirmation that the UK could continue to maintain its internal frontier controls at the frontier with other EU Member States.

2.11 The Amsterdam Treaty also provides for new arrangements, including the incorporation of the Schengen provisions, for co-operation in immigration, asylum, police and customs matters. The UK obtained various rights to opt into such co-operation in a flexible way so as to enable us to preserve our particular approach where necessary while also participating in those areas of co-operation which we judge important.

2.12   The Government will give careful consideration to the future exercise of these rights. In doing so we will take full account of three factors: the need to ensure effective co-operation within Europe in tackling organised crime (in which the UK has always played an active role); the need to preserve the UK system of frontier controls (as part of the Common Travel Area operated jointly with the Republic of Ireland, the Isle of Man and the Channel Islands); and the maintenance of UK control of policy on immigration and asylum.

Promoting race equality

2.13   The Government believes that a policy of fair, fast and firm immigration control will help to promote race equality. One of this Government's central themes is tackling the problems of racism and creating a society in which all our citizens, regardless of background or colour, enjoy equal rights, responsibilities and opportunities. The promotion of race equality has, therefore, been high on the Government's agenda since it came to power.

2.14   This is being taken forward in a number of ways already, which will develop and grow throughout this Parliament. In the Home Office this includes:

- consulting publicly on the Commission for Racial Equality's Third Review of the Race Relations Act 1976 and publishing a digest of other ideas received. The closing date for comments on both is 6 November;

- the introduction of specific offences of racially aggravated violence and harassment in the Crime and Disorder Bill;

- establishing the inquiry into the murder of Stephen Lawrence and the lessons which can be learnt;

- participating in a new Council of Europe group examining ways in which democratic states can best respond to movements, including racist and xenophobic groups, which threaten human rights; and

- setting up the Home Secretary's Race Relations Forum to give ethnic minorities a voice at the heart of Government. The first meeting of the Forum took place on 23 June.

2.15   Other Government Departments are pursuing many initiatives as well. These range from ensuring equality of opportunity in their own recruitment and employment policies (similar action is being taken by the Home Office) to improving access to public services for ethnic minorities.

Encouraging citizenship

2.16   One measure of the integration of immigrants into British society is the ease with which they can acquire citizenship. Acquiring a new citizenship is an important event. For both the individual and the nation, it brings new rights, new responsibilities and new opportunities. The Government believes that encouraging citizenship will help to strengthen good race and community relations. Accordingly, applications for citizenship should be dealt with more quickly.

3.1 Our current system of immigration control is too complex. In recent decades it has failed to keep pace with outside developments. Past attempts at change have been piecemeal. Typically solutions to a problem in one area have often created another elsewhere. Despite the professionalism and dedication of staff at all levels, the complexity of some rules, too many outdated procedures and chronic under-investment make it increasingly difficult for the system to deal quickly with those entitled to enter or remain and to deal firmly with those who are not. The Government does not underestimate the challenge which a complete overhaul of the immigration and asylum system presents. The issues are complex and, because of their impact on the lives of individual people and their families, extremely sensitive. Nevertheless, the Government is determined to undertake a comprehensive modernisation of our controls in order to deliver the fairer, faster and firmer policy to which it is committed.

Delays and backlogs

3.2 Large and persistent backlogs have been allowed to develop throughout the system:

- *asylum applications*: on 31 May 1998, there was a backlog of 52,000 asylum applications on which not even an initial decision had been taken. 10,000 of these applications were over five years old (see Figure E);

Figure E   ASYLUM APPLICATIONS [1] AWAITING AN INITIAL DECISION
AS AT 31 MAY 1998, BY YEAR OF APPLICATION

Total number outstanding - 52,110

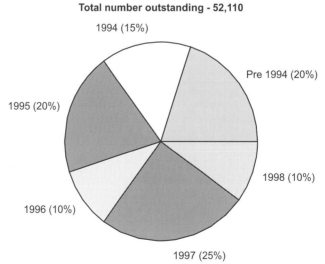

(1) Estimates rounded to the nearest 5 per cent.

- *appeals*: on the same date there was a backlog of 32,000 immigration appeals waiting to be heard. Of these, over 70% were asylum cases. In London, appeals can wait for up to 60 weeks for a hearing. Once heard, there can be a delay of up to three months for the adjudicator's decision to be communicated. Most applicants in the UK awaiting an asylum appeal have a vested interest in these delays;

- *citizenship applications*: on the same date, there were about 96,000 incomplete citizenship applications. Waiting times were about 18 months on average.

3.3   Delays and backlogs on this scale lie at the heart of the problem. They put unnecessary pressure on the staff who have to operate the system. They are not fair to genuine applicants who face long periods of uncertainty about the outcome of their application. They make it extremely difficult to deal firmly with those who have no right to be here. Tackling these delays and backlogs is a fundamental part of modernising our immigration control.

Costs

3.4   The costs of the present system are substantial and, unless something is done, guaranteed to grow quickly. The current cost of the control at ports of entry is about £120 million a year, but the estimated growth in passenger traffic suggests a potential funding requirement of around £150 million by 2001/02 unless a dramatic improvement in the efficiency of the operation of the control can be secured. In addition to volume growth, the nature of the challenge to immigration control is also changing. The substantial profits generated from organised trafficking in people enables criminal gangs to develop ever more sophisticated means of evading controls. If we are to respond to these challenges, we must be prepared to invest in more sophisticated methods of control.

3.5   But it is again the asylum system where the costs are greatest. It is estimated that the current asylum system costs the UK more

than £500 million a year. About £100 million is spent on processing individual applications. This includes the initial decision on the application, dealing with any appeal and the costs of enforced removals. But the bulk of the estimated costs, about £400 million, is spent on supporting asylum seekers, including direct support and other costs such as health and education. The current support arrangements are complex and expensive. Unless action is taken to rationalise those arrangements and deal with asylum applications more quickly, the costs of the asylum system are expected to almost double to £900 million within five years.

Inadequate control resources

3.6   Although some additional resources have been provided in recent years, they have not been sufficient to cope with the additional pressures on the control. The result has been the delays and backlogs already described. In relation to asylum, those backlogs have substantially increased the cost of the support arrangements for asylum seekers. Better resource planning and allocation to provide adequate resources for asylum casework would have saved much greater sums on support costs. We have to invest in order to improve the system, but the system itself must be made more efficient. A modernised and flexible control is needed to make the best use of available resources.

Outdated procedures

3.7   The previous administration failed to modernise and adapt immigration and asylum procedures in the face of changing demands:

- the legislative framework has not been adapted to enable the controls to be operated efficiently in the interests of the vast majority of legitimate visitors and to enable attention to focus on those who have no right to enter or remain;

- there are too many avenues of appeal which delay genuine cases and which are easily manipulated by those not entitled to remain here;

- there has been a lack of investment in technology which has prevented the development of new procedures at our ports of entry to cope with the increasing volume of passenger traffic and increasingly organised and sophisticated attempts to evade the control; and

- throughout the system, there has been a failure to establish coherent arrangements for the use of intelligence to enable resources to be targeted more effectively.

Complex procedures

3.8   The more complex a system of immigration control, the greater the risk of unfairness. Complexity encourages delay which can disadvantage the genuine applicant and be exploited by those wishing to abuse the system. And the more complex the procedures, even though they are applied fairly, the greater the risk that particular categories of applicant could be disadvantaged. The primary purpose rule was a good example. Immigration staff and the appellate authorities were required to make difficult judgements about the primary purpose of a marriage. It simply clogged up the system, diverted staff from more effective work and disadvantaged British citizens as compared with third country dependants of EU nationals to whom the rule did not apply.

3.9   The Government has already abolished the primary purpose rule. But we are determined to simplify procedures where possible and consider additional safeguards in some areas. Such changes will make the system more efficient and make it fairer. For example:

- the current "White List" accelerated appeals procedure is an unsatisfactory way of dealing with unfounded asylum applications from nationals of certain countries. It needs to be replaced as part of a comprehensive overhaul of the asylum and appeals process; and

- rather than tackle the complexities of the current system of immigration appeals, the previous Government decided to deny any right of appeal to visitors refused a visa. We believe that was wrong. A streamlined right of appeal would be fairer and would enable many citizens of this country to challenge decisions which prevent their relatives visiting them for important family and other occasions.

Piecemeal approach

3.10   The individual failings in the current system have been compounded by a failure to examine immigration control as a whole and its impact on other areas of public spending. Changes have been made in one part of the control without addressing the implications for the system as a whole. As a result, the changes have not worked because it has been too easy to exploit weaknesses elsewhere in the system, or they have simply shifted the problem from one area to another.

3.11   Previous attempts to restrict or remove benefits for asylum seekers produced an unplanned and unwelcome new burden on local authorities and local taxpayers. Because the previous Government did not seek a comprehensive and coherent solution to the provision of support for asylum seekers, local authorities had to pick up a substantial and growing bill for supporting those who were destitute. As well as being unintended, the burden has fallen disproportionately on those local authorities, particularly in London and, following the influx of Czech and Slovak Roma last autumn, Dover, who tend to attract a larger number of asylum seekers.

3.12   The piecemeal approach has produced a system of control which is unnecessarily complex. Delays in operating the system, and the numerous avenues of appeal once decisions have been made, mean that it is vulnerable to abuse. The following case study illustrates the problems:

Case study	
June 1985	Admitted for two months, subsequently extended to December 1985 to remain as a student.
December 1985	Application to remain longer as a student. Refused June 1986.
January 1987	Appeal against refusal dismissed. Further application to remain as student refused March 1987.
March 1987	Application for leave to appeal to the Tribunal. Refused.
July 1987	Asylum claim lodged.
October 1989	Asylum claim refused. Refusal papers undelivered as applicant had moved.
January 1991	Applicant traced and told to leave the country. Further application made to remain on basis of marriage.
May 1991	Application refused.
March 1993	Deportation notice served. Applicant appeals, renewing asylum claim.
September 1994	Asylum claim refused. Fresh deportation notice served. Applicant appeals.
August 1996	Appeal dismissed.
January 1998	Deportation order signed.
February 1998	Applicant detained and deported.

3.13 Without comprehensive change, there is a very real risk that the system will be unable to cope with future pressures.

CHAPTER 4

THE WAY AHEAD – AN INTEGRATED APPROACH

4.1   The failings of our current system of control demand that we adopt a new approach. We cannot continue to tackle each problem in isolation. This just shifts problems from one area to another, often increasing the overall cost to the public purse, without tackling the underlying causes of those problems. This would perpetuate the inefficiencies which, despite the commitment and hard work of immigration staff, have produced the delays and backlogs already described. And this would play into the hands of the racketeers and organised criminals who seek to exploit any weakness in our immigration controls for their own profit.

4.2   The only way of addressing the problems which this Government inherited was to undertake a fundamental review of the whole system of immigration control from start to finish, from initial applications overseas through to permanent settlement, citizenship or removal abroad. That is what we have done. Although that process has inevitably taken some time, it has confirmed the need for an integrated approach to maximise the efficiency of the system as a whole.

Review process

4.3   As part of the Comprehensive Spending Review process, there have been cross-departmental studies of the entry clearance operation; the system of control at ports of entry; and the asylum process, including the arrangements for supporting asylum seekers. In addition, although not formally part of that process, consultation documents have been issued following reviews of the asylum and immigration appeals system and the options for controlling unscrupulous immigration advisers. There have also been a number of other Home Office reviews, including one on all aspects of detention policy. The Government has also borne in mind the outcome of the Amsterdam Treaty.

Main themes

4.4   Each of these studies has identified strong links between different parts of immigration control and of the importance of examining the system as a whole. For example:

- pre-entry controls have a key role to play in reducing pressures on the port control and the asylum system;

- measures to deal with problems in a single area, such as asylum, are almost bound to fail. Those migrating for economic reasons simply try to exploit any other weakness in the system;

- there is a need for closer co-ordination within Government to establish and deliver objectives for the system as a whole;

- greater flexibility to target resources at key points would help to minimise costs for the system as a whole rather than simply shift the problem from one area to another;

- some problems, such as those caused by inadequately documented passengers, arise in different parts of the system. Devising separate solutions at each stage is wasteful and ineffective;

- making better use of IT would improve information flows throughout the system and provide new opportunities to integrate different parts of the control. The result would be a more efficient system for the genuine traveller and one less vulnerable to abuse; and

- more and better use of intelligence, including closer co-operation between the

various agencies, would help to target
resources more effectively at all stages of
the control.

The way ahead

4.5   The Government is convinced that an
integrated approach provides the way ahead.
It will enable the development of a more
coherent, more flexible, more streamlined
and more efficient control which provides a
better service and is capable of meeting the
challenges of the modern world. The
following chapters set out the Government's
plans to put in place an integrated and
modernised immigration control.

CHAPTER 5

PRE-ENTRY CONTROLS

5.1 Over recent years the contribution of the pre-entry element of our immigration control has become ever more important. It now plays a critical role in delivering the Government's overall immigration policy objectives. As the desire to come to the UK for economic betterment has increased, attempts to circumvent our control, both by individuals and by criminal organisations, have grown correspondingly. The large numbers of fraudulent claims and the use of forged and stolen documents are the visible evidence of an increasing awareness of how any loophole or potential loophole in immigration control may be exploited. These developments threaten to undermine the effectiveness of our immigration control as well as causing misery and hardship through the exploitation of vulnerable people.

5.2 It is therefore vital that we ensure that those passengers who have no claim to come to the UK are prevented from doing so. We rely heavily on an effective pre-entry control, with the use of visa and transit visa requirements, together with clear explanations of our policies in countries overseas. The entry clearance arrangements must also reflect the wider interests of the UK. We need to ensure that visitors, businessmen, students and others whose activities benefit the UK feel encouraged to come here. The Government is committed to ensuring that all those who have a genuine reason to come to the UK are allowed to do so with as little inconvenience as possible. Our commitment to maintain a fair, fast and effective entry clearance operation at posts overseas is based on that. We also recognise that many applicants have relatives who are settled here and wish under the Immigration Rules to join them. The Government intends to maintain high standards of service and ensure that procedures are fair.

5.3 For the UK, as for most other countries, visa regimes have become an essential part of immigration control in preventing the entry of inadmissible or undocumented passengers. At the same time, well managed visa operations can play an important part in facilitating the entry of the individual passenger. In 1997 entry clearance posts overseas issued over 1.4 million visas, more than 90% of which were processed in 24 hours, and many of these on the day of application. Obtaining a visa in advance can provide a basic assurance that the traveller is likely to be admitted to the UK, speeding up entry at the port, to the benefit both of the individual and of other passengers. The Government believes that there is scope for developing this process even further, so that the issue of the visa would be combined with the grant of leave to enter, subject only to an overriding power, for use only in clearly defined circumstances, to refuse entry to someone with a valid visa.

5.4 In recent years many countries, including the UK, have found that transit visa requirements have become increasingly necessary to close off loopholes in immigration control. The facility of allowing passengers to travel without a visa if they are in transit by air to a third country is open to abuse both by individuals and, more significantly, by racketeers and facilitators. In respect of the countries whose nationals feature most significantly in this abuse, transit visa requirements have unfortunately become necessary. The Government recognises the effect that these requirements can have on the commercial activities of airports, airlines and individual businesses. These concerns weigh heavily, and in relation to individual countries the Government will set them alongside the costs of allowing unauthorised people to come here with the intention either of making an unfounded asylum claim, gaining access to social security funds, or of working illegally. The Government will maintain the requirement for transit visas where on balance these are justified and extend them where the risk of immigration abuse is significant.

Entry clearance procedures

5.5   If someone is inadmissible to the UK it is in everyone's interests, including the traveller's, to decide this before they set out. Although the administrative costs of handling applications overseas are quite high (because it is expensive to post staff abroad), these costs are covered by visa and entry clearance fees. Moreover, preventing inadmissible passengers from coming here avoids the costs of dealing with a refusal case in the UK. These can include detention costs (in a small percentage of cases), removal costs, and the costs, which can be substantial, of financial support, health and education while the individual is actually in the UK. A balance has to be struck so that groups of passengers who are likely to be admissible to the UK are dealt with on arrival, but groups or categories which include a significant proportion whose cases are complex or who are inadmissible are pre-cleared through visa and entry clearance requirements. We do not of course apply visa regimes to all countries and we do not wish to do so.

5.6   In general, the entry clearance operation at UK posts overseas is effective, fair and efficient. But it must be responsive to changing needs. We have therefore reviewed the management of the entry clearance system to ensure much greater integration with other elements of the immigration control. A core element of the new approach will be a single management structure in the UK to manage the overseas operation, drawn from Foreign and Commonwealth Office and Home Office staff. We intend to exploit the

opportunities of up-to-date information technology so that the processing of entry clearance applications, and dealing with the applicant at the ports and after entry, can be done as swiftly as possible; and so that the possibilities of frustrating the control by destroying documents or using forgeries can be reduced.

A streamlined right of appeal for visitors refused a visa

5.7   The Government's manifesto commits it to introduce a streamlined right of appeal for visitors denied a visa. The Government proposes that this right of appeal should be restricted to those who wish to come to the UK to visit a family member but who are refused a visa to do so. Primary legislation will be required to provide this statutory right of appeal.

5.8   An appeal against a refusal to issue a visa may need to be heard quickly if it is to serve any useful purpose. For example, some applicants may wish to visit the UK to attend a wedding or a funeral, or some other important family event. An appeal which was heard after the event for which a visa was sought would be unlikely to be of any practical value.

5.9   A right of appeal would also need to involve an independent judicial element if it is to be seen as fair. The Government proposes to offer a choice between an appeal based on written submissions which would be disposed of quickly or an oral hearing of an appeal which would take longer to arrange.

5.10   There is no new money to fund appeal rights for visitors. The Government therefore proposes that those who wish to appeal against a refusal to grant entry clearance as a visitor should pay for at least part of the costs of their appeal. The costs will vary depending on the way in which the appeal is disposed of. It will still be open to an applicant to make a fresh application for a visa at any time.

Bond scheme for visitors

5.11   The great majority of those who apply for visas to visit the UK do so successfully. However, we are aware of concerns expressed about some refusal decisions which focus on whether a visitor is genuine and intends to leave the UK at the end of their stay. Entry clearance officers face difficult decisions in this area which inevitably involve a degree of subjective assessment.

5.12   One way of dealing with doubtful cases would be to test out the intentions of the applicant more strenuously by introducing financial penalties if conditions are not met. We have therefore decided to take powers to enable a financial bond scheme for visitors to the UK to be introduced. We shall start with a pilot scheme which will allow the merits of the scheme to be fully tested. Under the proposed scheme, if there are any doubts about a visitor's intentions the sponsor would be asked to deposit a financial security, which would be forfeited if the applicant did not leave the UK at the end of the visit. Such a scheme might provide a quick and simple route to a decision in cases of doubt, and an effective sanction against abuse of the visitor rules. It would not convey an automatic right to a visa and the entry clearance officer would still decide the application on the basis of the information available.

Strengthening the Immigration (Carriers' Liability) Act 1987

5.13   Immigration control has been under considerable pressure over the last ten years from an increasing number of inadequately documented passengers arriving in the UK. The Immigration (Carriers' Liability) Act 1987 was introduced to stem the flow of inadequately documented arrivals. Many carriers are now subject to large numbers of charges (currently £2,000 for each inadequately documented passenger) and the majority are therefore prepared to work closely with the Immigration Service with the objective of reducing the number. Among the steps they take are investment in training of their staff and the denial of boarding to passengers whose travel documents are not in order. Since the Act was introduced the Immigration Service has conducted over 450 training visits for around 150 carriers in over 90 different countries. Evaluation suggests an average reduction of at least 30% in the number of inadequately documented passengers they bring to the UK. The Government intends to develop this partnership with carriers to help them with their responsibilities under this Act.

5.14   The Government will ensure that the Immigration (Carriers' Liability) Act 1987 remains a central element of immigration policy and that it continues to be applied in a reasonable and effective manner. We extended its provisions in April to passenger train services from Belgium using the Channel Tunnel to reduce the large numbers of inadequately documented passengers arriving by that route. This worked very effectively and the numbers have now substantially reduced. We will not hesitate to take similar action elsewhere if necessary. We still face difficulties with passengers arriving from Paris on Eurostar services where legal difficulties in France have prevented us from extending the provisions of the Act. These questions are being urgently discussed with the French Government. The Immigration (Carriers' Liability) Act 1987 is an important and effective deterrent, although there have been some practical difficulties in its operation, in particular late or non-payment of debt by a few carriers. The Government is looking at ways of ensuring fuller carriers' compliance. This may entail reinforcement of the current legislation.

Other measures

5.15   Entry clearance and the Immigration (Carriers' Liability) Act 1987 are important to our immigration control. But their effectiveness has been undermined in recent years by racketeers and organised crime exploiting and facilitating economic migration by people who are not entitled to enter the UK. More sophisticated forgeries, an increasing trend for people to impersonate others, and increasing numbers of passengers destroying their documents just before their arrival in the UK, are all combining to counter the responsible attitude and diligent efforts by most carriers to prevent the carriage of inadequately documented passengers.

5.16 The Government intends to take a tougher approach to deterring and preventing the arrival of inadmissible passengers. It is easier and more cost effective to deal at source with abuse of our immigration laws and stem migratory pressures. Where problems arise suddenly in relation to particular destinations or nationalities, the Government will put in place pragmatic and speedy responses. These will include responding to potential immigration pressures by engaging Ministerial counterparts in the countries concerned; using radio and television networks abroad to correct any misconceptions that the UK is a "soft touch"; and regular and ongoing action at diplomatic level to ensure that other countries are fully aware of our determination to tackle abuse of our control. At the same time, the Government will draw to the attention of other Governments any issues which may be giving rise to immigration pressures or concerns, for example on the part of minority groups.

5.17 Immigration officials are often sent to other countries to liaise with carriers to stem the flow of inadequately documented passengers coming to the UK. Developing our intelligence system, and strengthening operational co-operation with other countries, will be important in helping us to identify trends and tackle trafficking. We shall also develop our approach to surveillance at ports of entry to facilitate the identification of inadequately documented passengers on arrival and to identify the inward carrier. For example, in collaboration with port operators and business partners, there has been a successful trial of the extended use of CCTV at Heathrow, and this will be further developed where it is likely to prove effective.

Airline Liaison Officers

5.18 One of the most effective preventative measures undertaken recently by the Immigration Service has been the placement of five Airline Liaison Officers (ALOs) overseas, working with authorities, carriers and the Immigration Services of other countries to provide advice and training to airlines, and to combat document and other frauds. International co-operation, in which ALOs have played a major part, has stopped several large groups of inadequately documented passengers from reaching Western Europe and North America: 120 were returned to their point of departure by the Cambodian authorities, 50 by the authorities in Lesotho. ALOs were also involved in preventing the attempted movement by sea from Africa of approximately 200 inadequately documented passengers. This group was eventually repatriated under the auspices of the International Organisation for Migration (IOM).

5.19 Despite these successes there were over 13,000 inadequately documented arrivals last year, an increase of 17% on the previous year. This trend continues upwards except in locations served by ALOs where the flow has been reduced. As a result of their work, around 1,800 inadequately documented passengers will have been denied boarding to the UK over the past year. It is estimated that this will have saved the welfare systems here in excess of £14 million.

5.20 The Government has, therefore, decided to expand the current network of ALOs. During the current financial year we plan to increase the network in six locations, selected on the basis of the number of inadequately documented passengers originating from or passing through them. We are currently discussing this with the relevant host Governments and airlines. In the longer term, probably by the end of 1999, we will wish to increase the network to around 20 ALOs, which will mean 15 additional posts in all.

CHAPTER 6

ON-ENTRY CONTROLS

6.1   The UK has always been a major centre of international trade and travel. That role has brought us many social, political as well as important economic benefits. It is essential that the controls at our ports of entry, which are fundamental to our whole system of control, should be fast, efficient and effective. We must be able to deal quickly with those who have a right to be here and genuine visitors, whether for business, study or pleasure, but be able to identify and deal firmly with those who seek to circumvent the control.

6.2   Over the past five years, the number of passengers arriving in the UK has increased by nearly 50%. Staffing levels at our ports of entry have risen by less than 10% over the same period and so processing that increase in the number of passengers represents a considerable achievement. The imposition of additional visa requirements has certainly relieved some of the pressure. In addition, there has been substantial investment to set up a computerised Suspect Index. This has helped to speed up the process of passenger clearance while strengthening checks for inadmissible passengers. But the Immigration Service has also introduced a range of efficiency measures in order to expedite the clearance of genuine passengers and make procedures as efficient and effective as possible.

Making better use of resources

6.3   There have been a number of initiatives to make better use of existing resources at ports of entry. They include:

- the introduction of new shift patterns to maximise staffing levels at peak periods;

- working in close partnership with carriers and port operators to improve the procedures for dealing with passengers;

- improvements in queue management;

- the introduction of assistant immigration officers to ensure that routine work is carried out at the appropriate level and to release more immigration officers for frontline duties;

- performance standards for passenger queuing times, published in national and local operating plans. The Immigration Service Ports Directorate has also developed mechanisms to monitor workload and quality of performance against its objectives, to help it focus on priorities; and

- a system to investigate complaints, overseen by an independent Complaints Audit Committee, which has helped identify and address procedural problems.

Better targeting of resources

6.4   As well as making the best possible use of existing resources, it is also essential that the maximum use is made of intelligence to target resources where they will be most effective. Initiatives of this kind which have already been implemented include the following:

- in April the Government reconfigured embarkation controls to provide an improved intelligence and target-led operation, using technology and involving a partnership between enforcement agencies, carriers and port authorities; and

- at Dover East a streamlined control is in operation to handle large volumes of EU nationals who arrive by car and on board coaches. Drivers of freight vehicles who are not subject to control are not systematically examined. Resources are focused on intelligence-led targeting of suspect vehicles to detect clandestine entrants. The result has been a substantial increase in the number of clandestine entrants detected.

6.5   These measures have helped the staff at our ports of entry to deal with more passengers and to increase control operations. As a result, it has been possible to meet most of the recently published service standards. But the volume of passenger traffic, and the demands from new airports and new terminals at existing airports, will continue to grow. Without modernisation and greater operational flexibility, so that resources are targeted more effectively on tackling abuse and clandestine entry rather than routine work, it will become increasingly difficult to maintain effective frontier controls, cope with passenger growth, deliver the kind of service standards that facilitate trade, tourism and education, and maintain the UK's position as an international hub.

Greater operational flexibility

6.6   The Government believes that greater operational flexibility is essential in a modern immigration control. Resources must be able to be deployed rapidly to areas of greater risk. Our current controls are based on the grant of written leave to enter or remain. The Government intends to retain the fundamental concept of leave and thus ensure all arriving passengers should continue to be seen by immigration staff. But there is scope to adapt the form and manner in which the control is carried out to improve its effectiveness. For example, there is no reason in principle, subject to safeguards (including data protection requirements) and availability of the appropriate technology, why there should not be an electronic record of leave to enter or remain rather than persist in every case with a system of stamps in passports which was designed for another age. Quite apart from new technology, there are also

opportunities to operate the controls more effectively by integrating the procedures so that the issue of a visa or entry clearance may also be treated as leave to enter, or by allowing multiple visits within the validity of a visa or for the period of extant leave previously granted. This will enable staff to be deployed from more routine tasks into areas of highest risk.

6.7   Our current legislation places too many constraints on the way in which we carry out our controls by specifying in too great a detail how those controls are carried out. It does not meet existing needs and will become much more inefficient as technology develops further. Our objective is to modernise the control by creating maximum flexibility. In the Government's view that is best done by retaining the requirement to obtain leave, but not necessarily in writing. Such action might include new powers to enable the Government to specify in secondary legislation the form and manner in which leave is to be given. Primary legislation will be needed for these changes.

6.8   Initially, these powers might be used to enable us to allow leave to be given by entry clearance officers; to allow leave to be used more than once (in the case of returning residents or those with extant leave); and to operate tour group and small ports schemes. In addition such powers would enable us to make further changes in future – for example, to enable us to exploit new technology. We propose to undertake further detailed examination of the feasibility of these options.

6.9   We also intend to take powers to require all carriers to advise the Immigration Service when they are carrying a third country national on a journey which ends in a small port in the UK (ie principally charter flights which are predominantly occupied by British citizens). We shall make sure that primary legislation gives sufficient scope to ensure that immigration controls can be modernised in the light of developments, whether technological or otherwise, consistent with ensuring that a firm control is maintained and that the essential requirements of fairness continue to be met.

Making better use of information technology

6.10 A modern and integrated immigration control must make the maximum use of information technology (IT). Information and intelligence gathered at one stage of the process must be available elsewhere in the system. Not only will this help to provide a better service by speeding the passage of those entitled to enter, but effective use of IT will enable better targeting of individuals and organised criminal groups who seek to abuse the system.

6.11 The Immigration Service has computerised some administrative processes, including checks against the Suspect Index. The computerisation of immigration, asylum and nationality casework, coupled with changes in working practices, will represent a major enhancement and modernisation of administrative and casework systems (see paragraphs 7.2–7.5). The Government believes that recent and future technological advances open the possibility of using IT to support the integration of pre-entry, on-entry and enforcement activity and to help modernise the labour intensive process of passenger clearance. One element of such an approach might be the use of automated pre-clearance systems. Accordingly, the Government intends to undertake a study of the available options. As part of that study, we will explore the potential for a private/public partnership for new capital investment.

An intelligence-led approach

6.12 Fundamental to the changes proposed in this chapter is the efficient use of intelligence to target resources. The current arrangements are too fragmented. The increased involvement of organised crime in immigration abuse requires a more sophisticated use of intelligence at all stages of the process. The Government will develop an integrated intelligence network that links and supports the pre, on and after entry control.

CHAPTER 7

AFTER-ENTRY

PROCEDURES AND

APPEALS

7.1 An integrated approach to immigration control requires that we modernise the after-entry control and procedures in parallel with changes elsewhere in the system. Just as at ports of entry, the after-entry procedures must provide a quality service to those entitled to remain and be able quickly to identify and remove those with no right to be here. This means:

- efficient and modern procedures for dealing with applications quickly;

- open and fair policies which sustain public confidence in the effectiveness of the control; and

- an appeals system which provides a fair opportunity to review decisions, but does so quickly and minimises the scope for abuse.

Modernisation

7.2 The Casework Programme is an IT-supported business change initiative whose aim is to modernise the way in which the Immigration and Nationality Directorate (IND) deals with immigration, asylum and nationality casework. Under a Private Finance Initiative contract which was awarded in April 1996, IND is working with a private sector partner, Siemens Business Services, to introduce fundamental changes in how the work is done. The organisational changes include a new "Integrated Casework Directorate" which will handle the casework which is currently the responsibility of five separate IND Directorates; a new Case Management Unit structure in which each unit will deal with a case from start to finish rather than continue the present narrow specialist approach; and a move away from the present hierarchical system of decision-making towards a more devolved structure.

7.3 To support these changes, we are planning to introduce a new computerised and integrated caseworking system which will replace the paper-based methods on which IND has relied until now. This will provide a single database of applicants' details and will mean that telephone enquiries can often be resolved without first having to obtain a paper file. Similarly, when action on a case passes from one part of the organisation to another it will no longer be necessary to transfer a paper file. This will offer substantial advantages in speed and security.

7.4 A "fast track" system will enable straightforward immigration cases to be dealt with immediately: the majority of these will be completed on the date of receipt. The new computer system will support caseworkers by providing on-line access to relevant legislation, instructions and guidance and will allow improvements in the quality control of the decision-making process.

7.5 Like almost any large new IT system the rollout of this important programme has been delayed, but when the new system is available it and the new ways of working will improve considerably the efficiency of IND's casework operations and the standard of service which it provides. The team-based working methods and the computerisation of immigration records will provide a basis for improvements in identifying fraud and abuse of the immigration and nationality processes.

7.6 The Government is also modernising other aspects of the after-entry procedures in order to focus resources more effectively. The requirement for foreign nationals to register with the police was originally introduced during the First World War as a wartime measure. It has been reviewed on a number of occasions since then. Following the most recent review, during which a range of interested parties were consulted, significant changes have been made to the scope of the scheme to reflect current requirements. These changes were implemented in May 1998. The changes focus the scheme more closely on those cases where experience shows that registration may perform a useful function.

Greater openness

7.7   The Government's recent White Paper on Freedom of Information underlined our commitment to greater openness. Individuals should as far as possible be given the reasons for decisions which affect them. The Government has already applied that approach to applications for British citizenship. Whereas reasons for refusal of British citizenship used not to be given, applicants will now always be told why their application was rejected. In addition, one consequence of the computerisation of immigration and nationality casework is that applicants will have rights under data protection legislation.

User panels

7.8   The Immigration and Nationality Directorate has made significant progress in developing a more open relationship with those who use its services, and in listening to their views. One recent initiative has been the establishment of the after-entry casework and nationality issues user panels, which have been in operation since October 1997. Sixteen user groups who have an interest in the service delivery aspects of IND's business and who have a national focus, are represented on the two panels, which meet quarterly.

7.9   The purpose of the panels is to consider the practicalities of what IND does, how it does it and whether the after-entry and nationality service provided is satisfactory. Recent issues discussed by the panels have included liaison between the Home Office and the Benefits Agency, handling of student applications and the implications of reconfiguring embarkation controls.

Immigration and Nationality Service Charter

7.10   As part of the Better Government initiative, discussions will take place with staff and user groups on the development of a charter for those coming into contact with IND on or after entry to the UK. Such a charter will need to address the responsibilities of applicants as well as setting out their rights. These might include the applicant's responsibility to provide full, accurate and true statements at all times and to notify IND of changes of address. The charter would also set out the standards of service that applicants are entitled to expect in return. IND will explore with the Foreign and Commonwealth Office whether the charter could encompass those applying for entry clearance.

Publication of caseworking instructions

7.11   We have made available to Parliament copies of the Immigration Directorates' Instructions (IDIs) and the Asylum Directorate's Instructions (ADIs), which provide guidance to IND staff on general immigration and asylum casework respectively. The IDIs are also now available on the Internet and arrangements are in hand to place a paper-based copy at various selected sites around the country. Other instructions on particular areas of the control will be made available shortly.

Fairer procedures

7.12   The Government is committed to a fairer immigration control. We have already abolished the primary purpose rule. The further changes which we have made, or which we intend to make, are as follows:

(i)   *Overseas domestic workers*

For too long there have been reports of overseas domestic workers being abused and exploited by the employers whom they have been allowed to accompany here. The

Government was determined to give these vulnerable people much greater protection and a status in their own right under the Immigration Rules. We worked closely with organisations which have campaigned for many years on behalf of these workers to devise new arrangements which would meet these objectives without, at the same time, opening up loopholes in the immigration control. We recently announced a new system under which the number of domestic workers allowed to come here with their employers will be significantly reduced, but those who do come will no longer have to stay with their original employer if they are mistreated.

(ii)   *Domestic violence*

The Government has been concerned about the situation of those who, having been granted 12 months' leave to enter or remain on the basis of their marriage to a person settled here, become the victims of domestic violence during that period. If they leave the matrimonial home they become liable to deportation and therefore feel themselves trapped in a violent relationship. We believe that the probationary year must be retained as an important safeguard against abuse of the immigration control. But in recognition of the dilemma in which such victims find themselves we are finalising the details of a concession under which those who are able to produce satisfactory evidence, such as a relevant court order, conviction or police caution, showing that they had been the victims of domestic violence during the probationary year, will be granted indefinite leave to remain outside the Immigration Rules. This will also be extended to those in a similar situation who have been given leave to enter or remain for twelve months under the concession for unmarried partners and to those whose spouse or partner dies during the initial 12 month period.

(iii)   *Unmarried partners*

Under the Immigration Rules, a person who is already settled in the UK may bring his or her spouse here to join them, subject to their ability to meet clear tests as to the genuineness of the marriage and the financial capacity of the couple. Without in any way diminishing the special position of marriage, the Government considered it unfair that unmarried partners in long-standing common law or same sex relationships should be completely prevented from being together. We therefore introduced a concession in October 1997 under which people in committed relationships akin to marriage may enter or remain here on this basis alone, provided they meet certain clearly established criteria.

(iv)   *Prevention of illegal working*

Under the present law, it is a criminal offence for an employer to employ a person who has entered or remains in the UK contrary to the Immigration Acts; or whose permission to enter or be here is subject to a condition prohibiting the employment. Experience has shown that, while this can be a useful tool, if targeted against unscrupulous and exploitative employers, there are some who are making more checks on potential employees than the legislation requires them to do in order to secure the statutory defence. This can lead to discriminatory recruitment practices which are unlawful under race relations legislation. The Government will take steps to re-emphasise to employers their duty to avoid racial discrimination in their recruitment practices when seeking to secure the defence under Section 8 of the Asylum and Immigration Act 1996. This could include, for example, a statutory Code of Practice. At the same time, the Government will strongly encourage the referral to the prosecuting authorities of cases involving organised racketeering and the exploitation of vulnerable groups of overseas workers for them to consider whether or not to prosecute under existing offences.

(v)   *Compassionate factors*

In many instances the compassionate factors in a case, particularly those concerning children, only come to the fore at the deportation stage. The Government believes there is scope for giving such factors a higher profile at every stage in the caseworking process. We are therefore developing criteria which would allow due weight to be given to any such factors in cases where refusal of leave to remain would otherwise be the appropriate course.

Overhaul of the system of appeals

7.13   The previous Government announced a review of asylum and immigration appeals in December 1996. The review is now complete and the Home Office and Lord Chancellor's Department published a joint consultation document about this on 13 July, with comments sought by 12 October.

7.14   The Government's view is that there continues to be a need for an independent review of the most adverse immigration decisions. The present system does not serve either the interests of appellants or of faster, fairer and firmer immigration control. The Government therefore proposes that:

● the present multiplicity of appeal rights should be reduced and;

● the structure of the Immigration Appellate Authority (IAA) should be radically reformed.

Both these proposals would require primary legislation.

7.15   The aim is to provide a single right of appeal to those who were lawfully present in the UK at the time of their application to remain in the UK. The appeal would be held quickly after the initial decision had been made and there would be no separate appeal against removal. There will also be a presumption of detention pending removal following dismissal of an appeal unless we are satisfied that the person will comply with instructions to leave the country voluntarily. Those who are removed administratively rather than deported would not face the same barriers to readmission.

7.16   The onus is on an applicant to make clear the grounds on which he or she seeks to enter or remain in the UK, including any compassionate factors. The Home Office would then consider whether the application met the requirements of the Immigration Rules and, if not, whether any compassionate factors, including claims on ECHR-related grounds merited an exercise of discretion in favour of the applicant. The intention is that this part of the process should normally be completed within two months. In the event of a refusal of the application there would, provided the applicant was lawfully present in the UK at the time of his application and in all asylum cases, be a single comprehensive right of appeal against the decision when these issues would be independently reviewed. The intention is that in most cases the appeal before the adjudicator should produce finality and that the entire process should be completed within six months. Where appropriate an applicant could be removed from the UK after this appeal.

7.17   The Government's view is that the present two tier appellate system is not working well. The main reasons are:

● differently constituted Tribunals of the IAA have produced determinations which are inconsistent and contradictory; and

● the Tribunal has often remitted cases to adjudicators which it ought to have decided itself, thus prolonging rather than bringing finality to the process.

7.18   There are two options:

● to restructure the Tribunal by changing its status and powers; or

● to consolidate the current two tier system into a single tier.

The Government's view is that the role of the Tribunal should be enhanced by changing its status and powers so that it produces an effective lead to the lower tier. The Immigration Appeal Tribunal (IAT) could become a court of record with the ability to create binding precedents. Appeals would be allowed to the IAT or a point of law. With the new ability of the Tribunal to create a body of precedent case law, the number of drawn-out cases should be significantly diminished.

7.19   The Government's consultation paper on immigration and asylum appeals also seeks views on a number of procedural issues such as the scope for shorter and more timely determinations, with a view to making the best available use of resources and reducing delay. The Government welcomes proposals for improving efficiency whether in relation to the particular procedural issues highlighted in the consultation paper, or other issues within the experience of respondents. The Government is particularly keen to hear the views of those directly involved in the process in an advisory, representative, judicial or other capacity and intends to find ways within the consultation period to promote dialogue and debate on these matters.

Control of unscrupulous immigration advisers

7.20   The Government is committed to controlling unscrupulous immigration advisers. These advisers exploit vulnerable people with promises they are often unable to deliver. The price their clients pay is poor advice or overcharging or both.

7.21   On 22 January the Home Office and the Lord Chancellor's Department issued a joint consultation document which sought comments on the kinds of behaviour to be controlled and the options for achieving it. Over 300 copies of the document were distributed to individuals and organisations. Of these, 53 commented on the document. A substantial majority agreed that the activities described in the consultation document were those which needed to be controlled. Equally, a substantial majority thought that a statutory regulatory scheme was the only way in which effective control of unscrupulous behaviour could be achieved.

7.22   The Government has decided to introduce legislation which would require non-legally qualified advisers, whether

offering advice in a voluntary capacity or for reward, to register with a regulatory body. The Government is considering the extent to which members of the legal profession should be subject to regulation in respect of advice of this kind and will announce its intentions as soon as possible. It is envisaged that any regulatory scheme will be self-financing with costs being met from registration fee income.

Legal aid

7.23   At present in England and Wales, asylum and immigration applicants can obtain legal aid in two ways:

- Green Form legal aid. This is intended to cover the costs of providing advice and assistance to applicants. Green Form legal aid does not cover the costs of representation; and

- certificated legal aid in connection with an application to seek leave to move for judicial review. Such applications may include challenges to an adverse decision made by IND, a determination of the IAA against which there is no right of appeal, or a refusal by the IAA to grant leave to appeal.

There is no legal aid for representation at appeals before an adjudicator or the Immigration Appeal Tribunal. However, the Government is providing funding of £5.9 million in 1998/99 to the Refugee Legal Centre (RLC) and the Immigration Advisory Service (IAS) to provide free advice, assistance and representation at these appeals.

7.24   The extent to which publicly funded advice and assistance is available in other EU countries varies, as does the form which such provision takes. In France, such support is available only to those who are lawfully resident, or in some cases to people claiming asylum.

7.25   For many years after the 1951 Refugees Convention came into force no legal aid was available to asylum seekers or more generally to people subject to immigration control.

Since the introduction of widely available legal aid there has been a very large growth in its use in the immigration field, with expenditure on Green Form legal aid amounting to some £26 million in 1996/97. There were also 1,925 applications for judicial review in 1997, the vast majority legally aided, yet in a substantial proportion of the cases leave to move was refused.

7.26   The Government is determined to bring this use of legal aid under tighter control. It cannot be right that legal aid is so freely available at the taxpayers' expense to those whose claim to remain in the UK is unfounded. The Legal Aid Board has published proposals to replace in the first instance the Green Form scheme for civil legal aid with a system of exclusive contracts, ie franchises let to individuals or organisations to undertake work at a fixed price. By this means there would be much better control over the provision of cases for advice and assistance and the quality and appropriateness of work undertaken. In examining these proposals the Government intends to look very carefully at their application to the immigration field, and will consider whether there are other measures which should be taken to ensure that public funds are not misused in support of deliberate abuse of asylum procedures and immigration controls.

7.27   In Scotland, legal aid for appeals follows the same general principles. However, responsibility for legal aid in Scotland will devolve upon the Scottish Parliament under the Scotland Bill and it will be necessary to consult the Scottish Parliament if the Government wishes to make adjustments to the availability of legal aid there.

Section 23 funding

7.28   Under section 23 of the Immigration Act 1971 the Home Secretary may make grants to any voluntary organisation which provides advice or assistance for, or other services for the welfare of, persons who have rights of appeal under Part II of the Act. The Home Secretary makes such grants to the IAS and the RLC. For 1998/99 the grant to the IAS is £2.7 million and to the RLC £3.2 million.

7.29   Under the terms of the Legal Aid Board's proposals for exclusive contracting it is open to the IAS and the RLC to apply for franchises to provide advice and assistance to asylum and immigration applicants. The Legal Aid Board's franchising proposals do not at present extend to representation. It will, therefore, be necessary to retain section 23 funding so as to enable voluntary organisations to provide free representation.

CHAPTER 8

ASYLUM PROCEDURES

8.1 The UK has a long-standing tradition of giving shelter to those fleeing persecution in other parts of the world, and refugees in turn have contributed much to our society and culture. The Government is determined to uphold that tradition. We will continue to observe with meticulous fairness our obligations under the 1951 UN Convention Relating to the Status of Refugees. We will also have careful regard to other instruments of international law protecting human rights to which we are a party. Primarily, these are the 1966 International Covenant on Civil and Political Rights, the 1984 UN Convention Against Torture and other Cruel, Inhuman or Degrading Treatment or Punishment, and the ECHR.

8.2 We supported a recent Council of Europe recommendation encouraging Member States to provide effective national remedies before removing a failed asylum seeker. We have participated fully in – and during the UK Presidency have steered – discussions aimed at improving the operation of EU asylum procedures, such as the Joint Position on the harmonised application of the definition of the term "refugee" in Article 1 of the 1951 UN Convention.

Supporting the voluntary sector

8.3 The Government at present provides approximately £3 million a year to voluntary organisations to assist asylum seekers on arrival and to help those who are granted refugee status. Unaccompanied refugee children are also given special assistance by a Panel of Advisers, wholly funded by the Home Office. The UK has also supported an EU resolution on unaccompanied minors who are nationals of third countries. The Government believes that the voluntary

sector has an important role to play in helping asylum seekers. The Government will continue to provide funds to national and regional voluntary organisations to assist in the settlement of refugees so that those given leave to remain may be empowered to lead useful, fulfilling lives and make valuable contributions to the cultural and economic life of the country. We intend to liaise with local authorities and others on what further measures might be developed to assist refugees and those granted exceptional leave to remain (ELR) to integrate into local communities.

8.4 Those granted refugee status or ELR may claim the Jobseeker's Allowance (JSA). Young people are eligible to join the New Deal for 18-24 year olds once they have claimed JSA for six months without success in finding work. Those aged 25 and over will be eligible for the New Deal for people aged 25 plus. The Government intends to put before Parliament Regulations to allow refugees to count the time spent on Income Support towards their eligibility for the Education and Training Opportunities available under the New Deal for people aged 25 plus. In both cases, discretion may be exercised to allow earlier access in some circumstances. Both of these New Deals will offer individually focused guidance to help genuine refugees find work or help them increase their employability.

A new covenant

8.5 The debate on asylum has been polarised between two extremes: those who oppose all immigration and those who oppose effective immigration controls. All asylum seekers are "bogus" to one group or almost all genuine to another. The real issue is how to run an asylum system which serves the British people's wish to support genuine refugees whilst deterring abusive claimants. The focus should be on creating an efficient system which does both, and one in which the responsibilities of both sides are set out in what amounts to a new covenant. This will involve the Government in recognising and fulfilling obligations to:

- protect genuine refugees by scrupulous application of the 1951 Convention;

- resolve applications quickly; and

- ensure that no asylum seeker is left destitute while waiting for their application or appeal to be determined.

In return applicants will be expected clearly to recognise their obligations, including to:

- tell the truth about their circumstances;

- obey the law;

- keep in regular contact with the authorities considering their claims; and

- leave the country if their application is ultimately rejected.

Our revision of asylum procedures is based on this recognition of mutual obligations – a new covenant.

An integrated approach

8.6   The fundamental flaw in previous attempts to deal with the substantial increase in asylum claims is that they have addressed the problems in isolation from the rest of the system. For the reasons explained earlier in this White Paper, the Government believes that it is essential that the procedures for dealing with asylum applications should be seen within the framework of an integrated immigration control. Potential abuse and exploitation of the institution of asylum harms the genuine refugee as much as it threatens to undermine proper controls on immigration. It is in the best interest of genuine refugees that there should be firm action to improve current procedures, including measures to deter or prevent from travelling those who do not meet the criteria for entry to the UK.

Faster decisions

8.7   The key to restoring effectiveness to our asylum system and to tackling abuse is swifter determination of applications and appeals. The Government inherited backlogs of over 50,000 cases awaiting decision and over 20,000 queuing for an appeal hearing. Some undecided cases date back to 1990 and appeals can take 15 months to list in London. Delays of this order send a clear message to abusive applicants that the system cannot cope and is ripe for exploitation; while those in genuine need of protection are condemned to a cruel limbo of worry and uncertainty over their future.

8.8   The Government will take strong and swift action to transform the asylum process:

- through reorganisation and computerisation of immigration, asylum and nationality processes as a whole;

- by investing more in the determination of cases to reduce the decision backlog to frictional levels by 2001;

- by investing more to reduce the number of appeals waiting to be heard;

- by streamlining the asylum and immigration appeals processes, consolidating multiple appeal rights into a single appeal right and strengthening the role of the Immigration Appeal Tribunal; and

- by transferring budget responsibility for asylum support to the Home Office and creating a wholly new and much more flexible inter-departmental planning and monitoring process to manage the system more effectively.

8.9   Delivering faster decisions is crucial to the success of the overall strategy. The Government is aiming to ensure that by April 2001 most initial asylum decisions will be made within two months of receipt and that most appeals to adjudicators will be heard within a further four months. Both these targets reflect average process times and the

Government expects that many cases will be dealt with more quickly. But achieving these targets will depend on a number of factors, including the successful implementation of the Casework Programme, the number of asylum applications outstanding which will be affected by changing international circumstances and the extent to which applicants and their advisers unnecessarily delay resolution of an application or an appeal. The Government will therefore keep these targets under review as the implementation of the wider strategy progresses. At present economic migrants abuse the asylum system because its inefficiency allows them to remain in the UK for years. A faster system with more certain removal at the end of the process will significantly deter abuse.

Legal representation at asylum interviews

8.10   The Government has considered whether in an asylum system geared to produce swift and fair decisions there is a need to make provision in all cases for legal representatives to be present at asylum interviews. It has concluded that legal representation at the asylum interview is not necessary to enable an applicant to set out his or her case truthfully. The asylum interview is essentially a fact-finding exercise to enable asylum claimants to say in their own words why they fear persecution in their own country. Whilst the Government neither encourages nor discourages the presence of legal advisers at the asylum interview, it believes that their presence is not essential to a fair asylum process so as to merit changes in existing procedures in this respect. It will, however, examine whether there is a need for the better provision of information for asylum applicants after interview on the availability to them of legal advice.

Post-interview representations

8.11   In a fair asylum process where speed of decision-making remains an important element both in identifying the genuine refugee and countering abuse, the

Government believes it is no longer justified in continuing to maintain the disparity in the time presently allowed after asylum interview for the submission of further material before a decision is made. At present this is 28 days for most port asylum claimants but five days for in-country applicants. The Government has decided with immediate effect to standardise the period allowed for all asylum seekers at five days. This will end the distinction between in-country and port asylum applicants; apply the same rule to all asylum seekers; contribute to the speeding up of the asylum consideration and decision-making process whilst allowing a reasonable period for further representations post-interview. Although the presumption will be that most asylum claims will be decided as soon as possible after the expiry of this five day period, discretion will be retained to permit an extended period where exceptional circumstances obtain.

Existing support arrangements for asylum seekers

8.12   The present support arrangements for asylum seekers have evolved through the charges to asylum seekers' entitlement to welfare benefit in 1996 and, for adults, the intervention of the courts following these changes. Under the changes to welfare benefits, help for asylum seekers was generally limited to those who apply for asylum on arrival at a UK port and only then until their asylum claim has been decided. People recognised as refugees or granted ELR have full access to the benefits system.

8.13   Those asylum seekers not entitled to welfare benefits under the 1996 changes were effectively put at risk of destitution until in October 1996 the High Court ruled that local authorities had a duty under section 21 of the National Assistance Act 1948 to provide care and accommodation to asylum seekers and appellants who were without any other means of support and who could, therefore, be considered to be a category at risk for the purposes of the 1948 Act. This was upheld by the Court of Appeal in February 1997. In

Scotland, a similar system of support has been provided by local authorities under section 12 of the Social Work (Scotland) Act 1968. Unaccompanied children, and families with children, have been supported under the Children Act 1989 and the Children (Scotland) Act 1995.

8.14   The result has been support arrangements which are messy, confusing and expensive, currently costing about £400 million a year and liable to rise to £800 million a year by 2001/02 if no action is taken to deal with the backlogs and delays in the process. The Court of Appeal judgment relating to the 1948 Act meant that, without warning or preparation, local authority social services departments were presented with a burden which is quite inappropriate, which has become increasingly intolerable and which is unsustainable in the long term, especially in London, where the pressure on accommodation and disruption to other services has been particularly acute.

Arrangements in other countries

8.15   The arrangements made in other EU countries vary widely, reflecting national differences in welfare provision generally and the number of asylum seekers in each country. It is, therefore, difficult to draw specific conclusions, although some general points emerge:

- a significant number of EU countries provide accommodation and other support in kind rather than by payment of cash allowances. In Germany, all benefits are paid in kind with a small cash payment for everyday needs. The Netherlands, Belgium and Denmark provide reception centre or similar communal accommodation for most or all asylum seekers. In Belgium, asylum seekers receive no support if they choose not to live in one of the centres;

- in countries where a cash payment is made, such as France and Italy, the period of payment is strictly limited; and

- in almost all countries, the provision for asylum seekers is separate from the standard welfare and other support for residents of that country.

8.16   At EU level, the Amsterdam Treaty provides for co-operation in the development of minimum standards on the reception of asylum seekers. The Government will participate in the development of such co-operation if it is in the national interest to do so.

Objectives for a new support system

8.17   In considering what form support arrangements for asylum seekers should take, the Government believes that they should satisfy the following objectives:

- to ensure that genuine asylum seekers cannot be left destitute, while containing costs through incentives to asylum seekers to look first to their own means or those of their communities for support;

- to provide for asylum seekers separately from the main benefits system; and

- to minimise the incentive to economic migration, particularly by minimising cash payments to asylum seekers.

Access to social security benefits

8.18   To deliver these objectives the Government believes that it must start from the position that people who have not established their right to be in the UK should not have access to welfare provision on the same basis as those whose citizenship or status here gives them an entitlement to benefits when in need. Any support for asylum seekers should operate on a separate basis, with provision offered as a last resort to those who have no other means including support from relatives or friends to which they can turn. The corollary of this is that asylum applications must be resolved much more quickly than at present, so that those who can establish an entitlement to remain in the UK are promptly distinguished from those who cannot.

Basis of a safety net scheme

8.19   Asylum seekers are temporary residents here and with few exceptions have no established residence status. Many should be able to support themselves, with help if necessary from relatives, friends and community groups, during the period when their application is being considered. Some, however, would be in genuine hardship if there were no publicly provided safety net. The Government is committed to providing such a safety net, but is determined to do so in a way which minimises the incentive for abuse by those who do not really need the support or who would make an unfounded asylum application in order to obtain the provision.

8.20 The Government has considered carefully the evidence, including that from other countries described in paragraph 8.15, about the best means of provision and in particular the relative advantages and disadvantages of cash-based support and provision in kind. Cash based support is administratively convenient, and usually though not inevitably less expensive in terms of unit cost. Provision in kind is more cumbersome to administer, but experience has shown that this is less attractive and provides less of a financial inducement for those who would be drawn by a cash scheme. The number of asylum applications fell by 30% following the withdrawal of some social security benefits in 1996, and despite a long-term underlying upward trend and the intervention of the courts in the 1948 Act case, remains at a lower level than in the year before the changes. Take-up of provision in kind offered under the National Assistance Act 1948 is estimated at 15% for single adults compared to an estimated 85% take-up of cash benefits by the equivalent eligible group.

8.21 The Government has therefore concluded that support for asylum seekers should no longer generally be founded on cash payments. Support will therefore be provided separately from the existing statutory benefits arrangements, and will be available only where it is clearly necessary while an application is awaiting decision or appeal. Accommodation, in such circumstances, will be provided on a no choice basis, with no cash payment for this purpose being made to the asylum seeker.

Other basic needs will also be met where there is a genuine risk of hardship, including food and other living essentials as well as facilities to enable asylum seekers properly to pursue their applications, for example by telephoning their representatives or travelling to attend an interview at the Immigration and Nationality Directorate. The Government intends to explore further the extent to which support of this kind might be provided through vouchers or other non-cash means, so as further to reduce the incentive to abuse of the asylum system.

How a safety net scheme will operate

8.22 The administration of a new support scheme for asylum seekers, entirely separate from social security benefits, will require new national machinery to plan and co-ordinate provision, obtaining information from around the country and purchasing places either directly or by contracting with local agencies. Asylum seekers would be expected to take what was available, and would not be able to pick and choose where they were accommodated, but where possible placements would take account of the value of linking to existing communities and the support of voluntary and community groups. An advantage of a national scheme will be the ability to plan strategically for such factors and to do so in consultation with local authorities, voluntary organisations and other concerned parties. This nationwide approach will help to relieve the burden on provision in London, where the majority of asylum seekers are currently concentrated. The budget and the machinery for administering it will be operated by the Home Office. The body responsible for obtaining and allocating accommodation would also be responsible for assessing whether applicants were in genuine need either by doing so itself or by contracting out the process to another agency. Provision would be made for a speedy independent review of decisions to refuse support.

8.23 The 1948 Act will be amended to make clear that social services departments should not carry the burden of looking after healthy and able bodied asylum seekers. This role will fall to the new national support machinery. The Government envisages that this will involve contracting with a range of providers to secure accommodation, including voluntary bodies, housing associations, local authorities and the private sector. The Government is particularly concerned to explore ways of harnessing the energy and expertise of voluntary and independent sector bodies in providing the safety net. Local authorities' current responsibilities to asylum seekers under the homelessness legislation will be removed and replaced by these new arrangements, but they will be expected to assist wherever possible (for example by making available any spare accommodation on a contractual basis). Where an authority unreasonably fails to co-operate the Secretary of State would, as a last resort, be empowered to direct the authority to provide information or accommodation (subject to appropriate reimbursement).

Families and unaccompanied children

8.24   Families and unaccompanied children account for a relatively small proportion of asylum applicants, around 15%. The Government will ensure that in providing a safety net for asylum seekers the needs of children are fully respected and their welfare and rights safeguarded. Appropriate access to education will continue to be afforded to the children of asylum seekers. Provision will continue to be made under the Children Act 1989 and the Children (Scotland) Act 1995 for unaccompanied children claiming asylum, but social services departments will no longer be expected to provide for asylum seeking families in the absence of special needs requiring a social services response. Where the need can be demonstrated, families will be provided with safety net support. The Government recognises that this will involve additional considerations to those which apply to single adults, and special care will be taken to ensure that provision for accommodation, clothing, food and other living essentials is sufficient and flexible

enough to support the children's well-being during the period when their asylum application is under consideration.

8.25   The Government accepts that some form of support should be available to an asylum seeker in need to the point where he or she has exhausted all appeal rights. But to continue support thereafter whilst the failed asylum seeker remained in the UK unlawfully would not be justified. As a general principle the safety net will not extend to such people, although as at present there will be measures to safeguard the welfare of children and other vulnerable persons.

Further consultation and strategic planning in the new arrangements

8.26   Considerably more detailed work will be necessary to set up the innovative arrangements which the Government proposes to introduce. The Government will consult widely with local authorities, the voluntary sector, community groups and other providers of accommodation, about the operation of the proposed arrangements. Once established, the arrangements themselves should derive the maximum benefit from the opportunity which a national scheme provides to develop a comprehensive and strategic planning approach. This planning process will also be carried out on a consultative basis, so that strategic decisions will be informed by the knowledge and concerns of those who will have a role in managing the outcome at the local and national levels.

Dealing with the asylum decision backlog

8.27   We cannot establish the new faster asylum process to which this Government is committed (see paragraphs 8.7 – 8.9) without first tackling the backlogs inherited from the previous administration. While large backlogs remain, abusive applicants will continue to believe that they can exploit the system. Backlogs and delays create additional inefficiencies in processing, and do nothing to foster the morale of conscientious caseworking staff.

8.28   In dealing with the backlog of cases it has inherited, the Government will adopt measures which are both firm and fair as well as promoting a faster process. There can be no question of an amnesty for those in the backlog. This would be unfair and would be seen as a reward for those who would abuse the system. Equally it would be unfair to ignore the consequences of very long delays, which are no fault of the applicant, in terms of the applicant's ties in this country or elsewhere. The Government will therefore adopt an approach in which the effects of long delays in reaching a decision will be taken into account and weighed with other considerations, but only in due proportion and in appropriate cases.

8.29   Such delay will not normally be a factor at all in the consideration of applications in the backlog dating from after 1995. Applications from before that date will be considered broadly in two groups. In certain of the very oldest cases, where an asylum application was made before the coming into force on 1 July 1993 of the Asylum and Immigration Appeals Act 1993, delay in itself will normally be considered so serious as to justify, as a matter of fairness, the grant of indefinite leave to enter or remain. This will not apply, however, to applicants whose presence here is not conducive to the public good (for example, on the basis of their conviction for a serious criminal offence), nor to any application for asylum made after the commencement of removal or deportation action against the applicant. Such cases will continue to be assessed on their merits without any presumptive weight being given to the delay in reaching a decision. Altogether in the pre-1993 Act group there are estimated to be a total of around 10,000 cases still outstanding.

8.30   For applications made between 1 July 1993 and 31 December 1995, estimated at about 20,000 cases, delay will not normally of itself justify the grant of leave to enter or remain where asylum is refused, but in individual cases will be weighed up with other considerations and, if there are specific compassionate or other exceptional factors present which are linked to the delay or which compound its effects on the applicant's situation, a decision to grant limited leave to enter or remain may then be justified. The sort of factors, which might be relevant here, not otherwise by themselves sufficient to justify leave to enter or remain, could include such things as the presence of children attending school or a continuing record of voluntary or other work by the applicant in the local community.

8.31   These measures will apply specifically and solely to cases awaiting an initial decision, and specifically and solely to applications made during the periods indicated. Refusal decisions already taken will be implemented with a view to removal or deportation in the normal way, as now, subject to the outcome of any appeal. New and recent cases will continue to be dealt with on the same basis as before, but extra investment in processing means that they will be decided faster than at present.

8.32   Under the previous administration, mountainous backlogs of asylum decisions were created and many old cases were not given the attention they deserved. We reject the concept of amnesty. This Government is determined to get to grips with the problem, and to tackle it with a practical approach which is fair to those who have suffered the worst delays yet firm with the most blatant abusers of the system. Above all the approach will look to the future, enabling resources to be kept focused on ensuring the delivery of an asylum system which is both swift and fair.

CHAPTER 9

IDENTIFYING THOSE IN

NEED OF PROTECTION

9.1   The system needs to do more to serve the very people for whom it exists: those fleeing persecution, torture and degrading treatment. Genuine refugees who arrive carrying a burden of fear and distress find their anguish compounded by the uncertainty of waiting in lengthy queues for a decision on their future; and that the public support they should expect has been undermined by abusive claimants. Tackling abuse will re-establish public confidence in the asylum system and support for helping genuine refugees. The measures which the Government will introduce to speed up the processing of all claims will benefit genuine refugees, and wherever possible these cases will be identified early and given additional priority. To that extent the human rights of genuine refugees will be recognised more effectively than they are now. That this has not always been the case in the past is illustrated by the following example:

Case study: **the applicant submitted his asylum claim in August 1995. He was eventually interviewed in connection with his application in September 1997. He said that he had been detained and ill-treated by the authorities in his country of origin on account of his involvement with a banned political organisation. Information provided by UNHCR confirmed that those who are considered to be active members of the organisation concerned may have a well-founded fear of persecution. The applicant was granted refugee status in June 1998.**

9.2   The Government is equally concerned that others in need of protection should have their cases promptly and effectively considered, and that safeguards are in place to ensure that their entitlement to protection is not overlooked. To reinforce this, it has given a commitment that an order-making power in the Human Rights Bill will be used to enable an asylum seeker whose application has been refused to appeal also on the grounds that his removal from the UK would breach ECHR rights.

Qualifying for settlement

9.3   Those granted refugee status or exceptional leave to remain (ELR) have to qualify for settlement. The Government has decided that with immediate effect the current four years' qualifying period for those recognised as refugees will be abolished in favour of the grant of immediate settlement, and those granted ELR having been refused refugee status will have to wait only four years instead of seven. These measures will help refugees and others granted leave to remain to integrate more easily and quickly into society, to the benefit of the whole community into which they have been accepted. They bring forward the point at which persons who would inevitably have been granted settlement achieve that status, at the same time making the policy fairer and swifter in application. The revised policy is wholly consistent with the Government's commitment to a more humanitarian approach to the UK's obligations under the 1951 Refugee Convention, and to faster identification of those in genuine need of protection through fairer procedures. Transitional arrangements for those with ELR who are already part way through the existing qualifying periods will seek to ensure that no one is worse off for having been granted a particular status sooner than others.

Well informed decisions

9.4   High quality information about countries of origin is vital to sound decision-taking. The Government has developed arrangements for this which are more systematic and more transparent. The Country Information and Policy Unit in IND has now prepared country assessments on the top 35 asylum producing countries in the UK. Copies have been placed in the House Library and will be placed on the Internet. The assessments will be revised and updated at approximately six monthly intervals. Each country assessment contains a bibliography of source material. The vast majority of the sources used are in the public domain and easily obtainable. They have been prepared to inform caseworkers taking decisions on asylum applications.

9.5   As part of the process of opening up the collection of country information used in assessing asylum claims, the Home Secretary has asked a group of practitioners, interest groups and officials – the Consultative Group – to consider, amongst other matters, the principles of country assessment and to seek to achieve agreement about core reference material, bibliographies and chronologies of events. The Consultative Group began meeting on 3 March and will report to Ministers later this summer. The Group are also looking closely at the model of the Canadian Immigration and Refugee Board documentation centre. The Group have been given copies of the country assessments as part of their remit to consider the format and collection of country information, and have offered initial comments on some of them. The comments centre on the content, balance and focus of the assessments and these will be taken into account in later versions.

9.6   Further systematic exchange of information between the Country Information and Policy Unit, other governments, government departments, international and non-governmental organisations will be developed consistently to inform the asylum determination process. The Government continues to participate at EU level in the work of the CIREA Group, which facilitates the discussion and exchange of expertise about country information.

Improving quality standards

9.7   As well as high quality, up-to-date and accessible country information, decision takers need clear guidance on the application to cases of the 1951 Convention and other criteria, in an organisational structure and culture that promotes personal responsibility, clear standards of performance and a commitment to quality decision taking. Much of this is already in place and the Government intends to build on the high quality and commitment already achieved. The IND Casework Programme aims to give decision takers greater personal responsibility, in addition to providing them with a wider context and range of work in which to approach asylum cases and a rigorous approach to quality review. Training and development opportunities will continue to benefit from the contributions of refugee groups and advocates. Fresh guidance has been prepared for caseworkers on deciding asylum applications, focusing on human rights issues and encouraging a methodical approach so that genuine cases whose strengths are less obvious on the surface are not overlooked. This guidance has been made public.

9.8   Evidence of torture will also continue to be taken very seriously. All asylum caseworkers receive training and instructions on dealing with applicants who are victims of torture. Training and guidance covers issues such as the UK's international obligations to victims of torture, the need for sensitivity when interviewing victims of torture and liaison with the Medical Foundation for the Care of Victims of Torture.

Fairer procedures

9.9   In reviewing asylum law and procedures, the Government is committed to ensuring that the necessary application of firm measures does not lead to, or rely on, actual or perceived unfairness. The Government considers that the so-called "White List" procedure, whereby most applications from certain listed countries are put into an accelerated appeal process on the basis of a country-wide assessment rather than the circumstances of the individual case, is an unsatisfactory feature of the present system and should be replaced as part of the wider overhaul of appeals in asylum cases.

9.10   The Government is satisfied that no unfairness has resulted from the operation of the White List power in practice, since the vast majority of applications from the countries concerned are unfounded and where special considerations arise these can be picked up through the individual scrutiny given by a caseworker or adjudicator when considering the question of certification. The Government is conscious, however, that there is a perception of unfairness in the use of a country-wide approach to designation. It considers that a better approach would be to replace the White List with arrangements to certify appropriate cases individually using the case-specific provisions for accelerated appeals in the current legislation, supported by the arrangements for improved and more discriminating country assessments which the Government has introduced. Until the new appeals arrangements are implemented, the Government intends to continue to operate the White List subject to due scrutiny of the circumstances of individual cases and the continuing review of conditions in the countries of origin of asylum seekers.

Chapter 10
Encouraging
Citizenship

10.1   In the UK "citizenship" normally means more than just the nationality of our inhabitants. It also encompasses elements of involvement and participation, and sharing of rights and responsibilities. Not all rights are dependent upon a person acquiring British nationality. Civil rights belong to all inhabitants, whilst political rights are enjoyed by British and Commonwealth citizens and, in some instances, EU citizens. However, the acquisition of the nationality of the country in which immigrants are living is a mark of their integration into British society. Our nationality legislation seeks to ease immigrants into acquiring citizenship by not placing unnecessary obstacles in their way. Applicants are not required to renounce the citizenship which they already hold in order to become British. Nor are British citizens required to give up their British nationality when acquiring the nationality of another State. By accepting the concept of dual citizenship, which we have done since 1948, we recognise that in the modern world, as well as owing an allegiance to the country in which they live, people also retain an affinity to the country of their roots. It is therefore possible to be a citizen of two countries and a good citizen of both.

10.2   Although we avoid placing unnecessary obstacles in the way of permanent residents who wish to acquire British citizenship, we do little positive to encourage such people to become British. The Government believes that more should be done to promote citizenship positively amongst the immigrant population, reflecting the multi-cultural and multi-racial society which we have become. However, people applying for citizenship currently have to wait too long for a decision. Quicker processing of applications would give a more welcoming signal to prospective citizens.

Nationality applications

10.3   In 1987, when the transitional provisions of the British Nationality Act 1981 came to an end, the Home Office received nearly 300,000 applications for British citizenship and average waiting times for processing these applications rose to a height of 36 months in March and April 1992. Waiting times then started to reduce, reaching 13 months in March 1995. However, since then they have started to rise gradually so that they are on average around 18 months at the present time. As mentioned in Chapter 7, nationality casework is included in the IND Casework Programme and will form part of the Integrated Casework Directorate. The efficiency improvements this will introduce will help to reduce again the processing times for applications, but a more fundamental difficulty is the inability to react speedily to a rise in the number of applications received, part of which is due to the way in which fee receipts are treated.

10.4   Applicants for British citizenship by naturalisation or registration pay a fee on application which ranges from £120 to £150. In past years, the numbers of applications received have outstripped the capacity of IND to deal with them and there is a large backlog – currently 96,000 cases are uncompleted. Intake is forecast to continue rising (from 59,600 in 1996/97 to 65,000 in 1997/98 and 70,000 in 1998/99). Waiting times will thus increase further despite process changes designed to reduce them. In view of the fee levels paid, this is impossible to defend. It is also inconsistent with our commitment to faster decisions.

Funding

10.5   Waiting times can only be reduced by applying more resources to nationality work and the Government intends to do this. As part of this strategy, consideration will be given to devising financial mechanisms which would allow the fees received from applicants in future to be better related to the resources allocated to processing citizenship cases. Together with the efficiency improvements mentioned above, this will mean that applicants will receive a better service than now.

Openness

10.6   On 22 December 1997 the Home Secretary announced that, notwithstanding section 44(2) of the British Nationality Act 1981, in future reasons would be given for refusing applications for British citizenship. Rather than operate a discretionary system in which some unsuccessful applicants were unaware why their applications had been refused or what they needed to do to make a successful application, there is now a more objective system wherein executive decisions have to be justified. That is a positive move. The Government has also set up a User Panel

with representatives of applicants for citizenship in order to improve the quality of service which we offer applicants by listening to the concerns of their representatives and discussing our procedures with them.

Residence requirements

10.7   Changes in the operation of the immigration control, in particular to introduce greater flexibility in the form and manner in which leave to enter is granted, may require changes in current residence requirements for citizenship under the British Nationality Act 1981. In addition, many of those who at present cannot satisfy the requirements are those who travel abroad on behalf of firms in this country to drum up business, and thereby contribute to the economic well-being of the country and help create jobs. The Government intends to create a more flexible approach to the residence requirements based upon whether an individual was ordinarily resident in the UK and paying his or her taxes here, the overall length of their residence and connections with this country, and the reasons for their absences.

CHAPTER 11
ENFORCEMENT AND
REMOVALS

11.1   Enforcement of the Immigration Rules is a key part of a fair and firm system. In fairness to those who have followed the rules and to deter others who might consider abusing the system, we must be able to identify and deal appropriately with those in the UK without authority. There will always be some people who, despite having exhausted the appeals machinery, still refuse to leave voluntarily.

11.2   The growth in immigration racketeering also requires a new approach to enforcement at national and international level. We must be able to identify and disrupt the organisers who make huge profits from exploiting economic migrants. Tackling racketeering requires a co-ordinated multi-agency and international approach with a structure to enable intelligence to be properly developed. Historically, the Immigration Service has not needed to develop such a structure, and its enforcement policy has concentrated on the illegal entrants rather than the racketeers. Such an approach is no longer adequate to stem the tide. Criminal groups see illegal immigration as an easy source of income. International co-operation between the police and immigration authorities will be increasingly important if racketeers are to be disrupted. Against this background, the Government intends to take a number of steps to strengthen the enforcement effort as part of the integrated approach to immigration control.

Preventing abuse

11.3   The Government is determined to stamp out the blatant and often cynical abuse that clogs up the system with hopeless cases and unnecessary appeals. The existing criminal offences directed at those who seek or obtain leave to enter or remain by deception will be extended and strengthened. Failed asylum seekers whose claims have involved blatant deceit will be liable to prosecution in appropriate cases. The criminal law has a role to play in stamping out abuse of immigration control.

Bogus marriages

11.4   Our Immigration Rules relating to marriage are designed to prevent abuse by those who are prepared to enter into marriage simply as a means to obtain settlement. Nevertheless, there is ample evidence to show that large numbers of bogus marriages are being contracted in the UK every year. A bogus marriage is one arranged for the sole purpose of evading statutory immigration controls; typically a marriage of a person from a non EU country (who does not otherwise qualify to remain in the UK) to a British citizen, an EU national or a person settled here.

11.5   The Government is determined to take steps to eradicate this abuse of the immigration system. The Immigration Service has intensified efforts recently to prosecute both the racketeers organising bogus marriages and the individuals involved. But the Government believes that further measures are needed and proposes to enhance the statutory powers of registrars on the lines recommended in the White Paper "Registration: Proposals for Change". One of the proposals in the White Paper which has been outstanding since 1990 was that registrars should be given a statutory power to call for documentary evidence of age, identity and marital status. This was with a view to establishing that couples are free and eligible to contract a valid marriage in England and Wales.

Multi-agency co-operation

11.6 Immigration-related crime crosses many barriers – benefit and housing fraud, unlawful employment, illegal activities linked to prostitution, rackets involving asylum claims and marriages, student loan fraud, passport and document abuse. Immigration crime generates huge sums for criminal organisations and facilitates other criminal activities, such as drug trafficking and money laundering. It exploits the vulnerable: those who enter clandestinely are unable to defend themselves against further exploitation, and many become victims of extortion. To combat this crime more effectively, the Government is developing a more proactive approach to intelligence and inter-agency co-operation.

11.7 In November 1997, the National Criminal Intelligence Service (NCIS) established an Organised Immigration Crime Section. It is currently engaged in a number of projects targeting the criminal networks involved in bringing illegal immigrants to the UK. The Section works alongside other specialist units with officers from the Benefits Agency, Customs and the Security Services in order to maximise each other's knowledge and skills. It is in the forefront of the Government's development of a more pro-active, intelligence-led approach to combatting the problem, including improved co-operation with our European partners. Information from Europol feeds through to the Unit via the UK's Europol National Unit at NCIS.

11.8 A multi-agency approach to combatting immigration crime is vital. Joint operations between the Immigration Service and other agencies targeting benefit and housing fraud by illegal entrants and exploitation by unscrupulous employers have proved cost-effective and successful exercises. More are required. The recent inter-departmental working party, led by the Ministry of Agriculture, Fisheries and Food, targeting gangmasters who provide illegal labour to the farming industry, is a good example of Departments working together towards a common goal.

Additional powers for immigration officers

11.9 Full commitment to multi-agency co-operation does not exclude independent operational efficiency. At present, immigration officers must rely upon the police to carry out a number of tasks during the process of immigration law enforcement. The police involvement stems largely from the fact that certain powers are vested in the police and not in immigration officers. Enforcement operations can therefore sometimes become unwieldy and inefficient in terms of resource deployment. Supporting the Immigration Service in its operation to arrest and detain those who have deliberately absconded in order to avoid removal represents a substantial burden on police time. Concerns have been expressed about the impact on communities of uniformed police officers taking part in removals. The enforcement effort would be strengthened if immigration officers, who do not wear uniforms, had greater powers to conduct operations against immigration offenders in consultation with the police but without their direct involvement in every case. Dispensing with the services of the police where they have traditionally been employed is by no means unprecedented. Other agencies, such as Customs and Excise, the Benefits Agency and the Post Office have for some time now been exercising powers of their own independently and are good examples of how traditional police work can be taken on sensitively. Training commensurate with the needs would, of course, need to be provided. It is not the intention that the Immigration Service becomes an independent "immigration police" force. The measures outlined below do not go beyond the response to a perceived need. Rather, they are a carefully targeted approach to the more effective use of resources in a way which will provide the tools immigration officers need to enforce the law.

11.10   The immigration officer's powers of arrest derive from the Immigration Act 1971 and the Asylum and Immigration Act 1996. They allow immigration officers to effect arrests, without warrants, for specific immigration offences and to effect detention under the 1971 Act. They have not been used routinely as attendant powers of search and entry, comparable to those held by the police and customs officers, are not held by immigration officers. An immigration officer can arrest a suspected offender but has limited ability to search the person and the premises where the arrest took place without the person's permission. Arresting without appropriate powers of search raises important safety concerns and evidence relating to the subject's status and identity may go unfound. At present, the police are asked to effect the arrest and conduct a search, using their powers under section 32 of the Police and Criminal Evidence Act 1984 (PACE).

11.11   Further difficulties arise when a suspected immigration offender is identified but refuses access. A police officer can enter the premises and conduct a search without a warrant if the offence is an arrestable offence under the provisions of PACE. "Facilitation" is the only such immigration-related "arrestable offence". For any other immigration offence a warrant is required if entry is denied. Warrants can be obtained by immigration officers, but not in all circumstances, and even when obtained *must* be executed by police officers.

11.12   The Government proposes, therefore, to extend the immigration officer's existing powers of arrest and provide powers in the area of search, entry and seizure. We will be considering the scope for the execution of warrants by immigration officers without a police presence. In addition, we shall consider whether we can bring about improvements in the prosecution process for immigration offences, including a more proactive role for the Immigration Service. The Government is well aware of the sensitivities of the ethnic minority communities to the handling of immigration matters and will ensure that appropriate and adequate training is provided to immigration officers about any extension of their existing powers.

Better use of resources

11.13   Over 80% of failed asylum seekers live in the Metropolitan area of London. Enforcement resources are therefore concentrated in the South East. But if the asylum support arrangements proposed earlier in this White Paper achieve a wider geographical distribution and if more absconders seek work elsewhere, the need for a greater and more visible presence in the provinces will increase. The spread of resources around the country was the subject of a wide-ranging review in 1997 which has led to the redeployment of a number of posts to other major metropolitan areas in Manchester, Glasgow, Leeds and Bristol.

Fingerprinting

11.14   An effective identification system is an essential element of an effective removals strategy. The current system is aimed at deterring multiple asylum applications and, hence, widespread benefit fraud. However, the current systems were set up in haste and are limited in their effectiveness. The technology in use is outdated and difficult to sustain. It barely copes with present demands and is inadequate to meet any additional requirements. Under present legislation, immigration officers are empowered to take fingerprints of all those who are detained while liable to examination or removal, in order to establish their identity. Under the Asylum and Immigration Appeals Act 1993, all asylum applicants can be fingerprinted.

11.15   The system is outdated and requires investment before it can add significantly to the removals effort. We will be considering the extent to which the use of targeted fingerprinting with commensurate technical support would substantially strengthen the enforcement effort. The protocol to the Eurodac Convention referred to later in this chapter will, in any event, require a change to our existing legislation to provide for the routine fingerprinting of certain illegal immigrants.

Documentation

11.16   The documenting of people we seek to remove who have destroyed all earlier documents presents a significant barrier in the removals process. In the majority of cases the Immigration Service can remove persons using a standard format EU travel letter. However, some countries only permit the use of their national documents: this leads to delays which can run to six months or more. It is often the case that those nationalities that produce the greatest pressure on our immigration control are also those for whom such national documents must be obtained.

11.17   Where an approach has to be made to a high commission or embassy it is necessary to support the application with proof of the person's identity. This can be difficult to obtain without the co-operation of the individual concerned. Where nationality is disputed or supporting documentation cannot be obtained it can prove impossible to elicit a document.

11.18   The Immigration Service has instituted a number of initiatives to help overcome these problems. These include a scheme to apply for documents earlier in the consideration process and direct contacts with representatives of the countries with whom difficulties about documentation have arisen. We are also in the process of establishing a dedicated unit tasked with obtaining documents for the Immigration Service as a whole.

Readmission agreements

11.19   The UK has not in the past negotiated any readmission agreements with third countries. Historically, we have not seen formal readmission agreements as an aid to returning failed asylum seekers or illegal immigrants because they can introduce an extra level of bureaucracy and the time taken

to negotiate readmission agreements can be considerable. Instead, we have preferred to effect removals through bilateral contacts and in line with established international practice.

11.20   However, internationally there is an increasing use of readmission agreements. Experience of other countries has been that a mixture of compulsory and voluntary returns through negotiated agreements can work well. Experience among EU Member States has been of particular relevance. We are examining whether we should actively be seeking such agreements with a range of third countries.

11.21   Readmission agreements will also act to facilitate the provision of documents to people who have no documentation and where it has proved time consuming and costly to establish their identity and nationality. This is an area in which the difficulty in effecting returns is the subject of continuing discussions in the EU and which we particularly promoted during the UK Presidency of the EU.

Voluntary returns

11.22   As in the case with readmission agreements, the UK has not previously seen voluntary return agreements as an integral part of its immigration policy. The experience of other countries has been that a mixture of compulsory and assisted voluntary returns through negotiated agreements, often working through non-governmental organisations, has worked well. Exchanges at EU level have provided useful information about other Member States' practices in this area. Voluntary return programmes of other countries are designed to effect the return of certain categories of people, including those who have applied for asylum or have had such applications refused, who have decided that they wish to return to their countries of origin but who are either lacking accurate information about the situation in their home countries or the means to give effect to their wishes.

11.23   We are examining the issues involved in voluntary return programmes and will, in particular, consider whether running a pilot study for the return of those who are liable to removal would help assess the benefits of such programmes. Such a pilot study might involve an international migration organisation administering a small fund to assist the voluntary return of asylum seekers.

The Dublin Convention

11.24   In some cases it is appropriate for an asylum seeker to be returned to a safe third country without their claim for asylum being examined here. Last year over 1,000 asylum seekers were returned to safe third countries; the great majority to EU Member States.

11.25   The Dublin Convention was signed by the then UK Government in 1990. The Convention came into force on 1 September 1997, since when it has governed arrangements for safe third country cases in the EU. The basic principle underlying the Convention is that asylum claims should be examined just once in the EU and that the Member State responsible for the presence of the asylum seeker in the EU should be responsible for conducting that examination, wherever the claim is made. It also aims to prevent asylum seekers being passed between several Member States without any taking responsibility for examining the claim, and to deal with the problem of asylum seekers claiming asylum in a number of Member States.

11.26   It is necessary in individual cases to establish sufficient evidence to satisfy a Member State that it is responsible according to the Convention criteria (for instance the point at which they entered the EU or the place they first claimed asylum). Asylum applicants cannot be transferred to another Member State until the State in question has accepted responsibility.

11.27   There is a common appreciation among most EU Member States that the Convention is not working as it should. Far too few asylum cases in the EU are coming within the scope of the Convention. The Convention is particularly difficult to apply in circumstances where the asylum seeker is undocumented and is unable or unwilling to provide information which would help establish that another Member State is responsible.

11.28   The Government made the operation of the Convention a key priority for the UK's Presidency of the EU, which ended in June 1998. The Government secured agreement to a comprehensive programme of action designed to improve the operation of the Convention and is committed to continue work with our European partners in that task.

11.29   Those asylum seekers whose claims are to be transferred to another Member State are entitled under section 2 and 3 of the 1996 Act to appeal against the decision only after they have left the UK. The only way such a decision may be challenged before the applicant is transferred is by means of a judicial review application. At present, a significant proportion of asylum seekers who are to be transferred under the Dublin Convention make such applications, thus substantially delaying their transfer.

11.30   Such applications are frustrating the proper transfer of asylum seekers to other EU Member States. In a large number of cases these are applicants who have had their claims considered and rejected in another Member State and in others they are persons who have had ample opportunities to register claims in another Member State. The Government believes that it is important that such asylum seekers are transferred quickly. This is necessary both as a deterrent to abusive or unfounded applicants and to ensure that those in need of protection have their claims considered as soon as possible. The Government does not favour the introduction of suspensive appeals in these cases but is considering the options, including amendment of current legislation, to enable asylum seekers whose claims are properly the responsibility of other EU Member States to be transferred more quickly.

Co-operation on fingerprinting

11.31   Another of the main priorities of our Presidency was to take forward work on developing a legal framework for a central database of fingerprints to support the operation of the Dublin Convention. The Eurodac Convention, when signed and ratified, will create a computerised central database which will allow the comparison of the fingerprints of asylum seekers across the EU. If a fingerprint match is found as a result of a comparison in the central Eurodac database the Member States concerned will then enter into bilateral discussions under the terms of the Dublin Convention.

11.32   Although final agreement to the draft Eurodac Convention was not achieved at the Justice and Home Affairs Council in May, EU Ministers did agree that a protocol to the draft Convention should be developed to extend the scope of the fingerprinting requirement to include certain categories of illegal immigrants where to do so would be relevant in supporting the operation of the provisions of Dublin. Ministers agreed that the protocol should be ready for signature by the end of the year. Those whose fingerprints would be included in the central database as a result of such a protocol would be those who are identified as having illegally crossed the external borders of the EU. There would only be a requirement to take fingerprints if the person was identified as an illegal entrant in the Member State via which he or she had entered the EU. The Government accepts that such an extension of the scope of the Eurodac Convention should further enhance the operation of the Dublin provisions.

CHAPTER 12
DETENTION

12.1 Effective enforcement of immigration control requires some immigration offenders to be detained. At any one time, only about 1.5% of those liable to detention under immigration powers are actually detained. The statutory provisions for immigration detention are found in the Immigration Act 1971 and the Immigration (Places of Detention) Direction 1996. A person may principally be detained in the following circumstances under immigration law:

a) as a passenger who is required to submit to further examination, pending a decision to give or refuse leave to enter; or

b) as a person who has been refused leave to enter or who is an illegal entrant, pending the setting of removal directions and removal; or

c) if he has been recommended for deportation by a court and is detained pending the making of a deportation order in pursuit of the court recommendation; or

d) if he has been given notice of the intention to deport him, pending the making of a deportation order; or

e) if he is the subject of a deportation order pending his removal or departure from the UK.

Under the Immigration (Places of Detention) Direction 1996 persons may be detained inter alia in:

● secondary examination areas at ports;

● Prison Service establishments;

● Immigration Service detention centres; and

● police cells.

Additionally, a person is in lawful custody when he is being escorted inter alia to or from a place of detention.

12.2 A comprehensive review of detention was commissioned by the Government in August 1997. This review was conducted internally within the Home Office, but views were taken from all the main interest groups, and account was taken of the recommendations from reports by Sir David Ramsbotham, Her Majesty's Chief Inspector of Prisons, on Tinsley House and Campsfield House detention centres.

Detention criteria

12.3 It is regrettable that detention is necessary to ensure the integrity of our immigration control. The Government has decided that, whilst there is a presumption in favour of temporary admission or release, detention is normally justified in the following circumstances:

● where there is a reasonable belief that the individual will fail to keep the terms of temporary admission or temporary release;

● initially, to clarify a person's identity and the basis of their claim; or

● where removal is imminent.

In particular, where there is a systematic attempt to breach the immigration control, detention is justified wherever one or more of these criteria is satisfied.

12.4 The Government also recognises the need to exercise particular care in the consideration of physical and mental health when deciding to detain. Evidence of a history of torture should weigh strongly in favour of temporary admission or temporary release whilst an individual's asylum claim is being considered.

12.5 The detention of families and children is particularly regrettable, but is also sometimes necessary to effect the removal of those who have no authority to remain in the UK, and who refuse to leave voluntarily. Such detention should be planned to be effected as close to removal as possible so as to ensure that families are not normally detained for more than a few days.

12.6 Unaccompanied minors should never be detained other than in the most exceptional circumstances and then only overnight with appropriate care if they, for example, arrive unaccompanied at an airport. Where they cannot be cared for by responsible family or friends in the community, they should be placed in the care of the local authority whilst the circumstances of their case are determined. But the age of a person is not easily determined in every case. This is especially so where individuals enter the country with documents which suggest that they are an adult and later claim to be a minor. Sometimes people over 18 claim to be minors in order to be released from detention. In all cases, people who claim to be under the age of 18 are referred to the Refugee Council Children's Panel. Where reliable medical evidence indicates that a person is under 18 years of age they will be treated as minors and will therefore not normally be detained.

Reasons for detention

12.7 The Government is satisfied that the decision to detain should remain one for the Immigration Service, against the above criteria. Written reasons for detention should be given in all cases at the time of detention and thereafter at monthly intervals, or at shorter intervals in the case of detained families. Taking into account that most people who are detained are held for just a few hours or days, initial reasons will be given by way of a check list similar to that used for bail in a magistrates' court.

Judicial element in the detention process

12.8 Many more people fit the criteria for detention than are currently held. There is no reason to believe that the administrative process has led to people being improperly detained. Nonetheless, the Government believes that there should be a more extensive judicial element in the detention process. It is proposed that the judicial element should be by way of bail hearings about seven days after initial detention, followed by a further hearing for those not granted bail on the first occasion. We will consult with the judicial authorities and others on the detail of this proposal. It is not straightforward and will have considerable resource implications as, on present volume, about 200 bail hearings a week would need to be managed.

12.9 It is envisaged that in addition to judicial hearings the existing facility for chief immigration officers to grant bail would be retained. The present right to apply for bail to an Immigration Appeals Adjudicator (used on average about 120 times a month) would need to be modified or subsumed into any new system.

12.10 In addition to any consideration of bail through the judicial process, the Immigration Service will continue its periodic administrative review of detention in each case. Individuals should only be detained where necessary.

Length of detention

12.11 Detention should always be for the shortest possible time, but the Government is satisfied that there should be no legal maximum period of detention. Timing of detention to facilitate removals of those unwilling to depart voluntarily is not easy, because of last minute delays caused by further representations. Often detainees are held for longer periods only because they decide to use every conceivable avenue of multiple appeals to resist refusal or removal. A balance has to be struck in those circumstances between immediately releasing the person and running the risk of encouraging abusive claims and manipulation. The measures proposed earlier in this White Paper, to reduce process delays, should reduce the incidence of this sort of circumvention of the control.

Places of detention

12.12   The Government has welcomed the views of Her Majesty's Chief Inspector of Prisons and others and, as resources become available, is committed to pursuing a strategy of detaining in dedicated detention and holding centres, not prisons. About half of those currently detained are held in Prison Service establishments. Most of these (350) are in the specially dedicated immigration units at Haslar and Rochester.

12.13   It is likely that even in the long term, for reasons of geography, security and control, a number of detainees will need to be held in prisons. However, use of detention centres is preferable to prisons in the vast majority of cases and, in principle, the Government prefers to use detention centres. Where prison establishments hold significant numbers of immigration detainees in specialist units, we try to ensure that facilities mirror the more relaxed regimes in detention centres.

12.14   Consideration of the provision for immigration detention centres will take account of the need to use prison less, to provide for men, women and discrete family units and, in all cases, to ensure effective health, safety and control. Whilst recognising the need to ensure the current number of places are efficiently used, the Government is considering the need for an increase in the detention estate to facilitate an effective immigration control and the removal of those with no authority to remain in the UK.

Statutory rules

12.15   Immigration detention centres have evolved over a number of years. They are managed under contract between the Government and the private sector. The contract documents set out the requirements and performance standards. These have been refined and, over time, have established a greater degree of continuity of approach.

12.16   The Government accepts that detention centres must be put on a better footing and within a statutory framework. We note particularly Sir David Ramsbotham's view that the safety of centres requires there to be a system of rules and sanctions which are clearly understood and, preferably, set out in a compact – an "agreement" between detainees and the contractor on behalf of the State.

12.17   It is, therefore, proposed to seek powers for statutory rules covering all aspects of the management and administration of detention centres. These will regulate the rights and responsibilities of detainees and of those who manage detention centres.

12.18   Publication of more information about detention centre contracts is envisaged subject to withholding only those details which are commercially confidential. Only a very small part of the material in these contracts is of commercial significance and the rest should be in the public domain. That will be made clear in the negotiation of any new contracts for detention centres.

Powers of detention

12.19   At present contractors' staff derive their authority from the Immigration Acts, Criminal Law Act 1967 and Public Order Act 1986. Whilst these statutes are sufficient for lawful execution of their duties, it would be helpful for the powers of detention custody officers to be set out on the face of a single statute. The Government therefore proposes to seek specific powers for detention custody officers who work in detention centres similar to those provided for prisoner custody officers who work in the privately managed prisons. Such powers would cover the use of force and search powers.

12.20   In pursing these improvements to the use and management of detention, the Government is mindful that the deprivation of liberty is a grave step which must only be used with great care and when no alternative ways of ensuring compliance are likely to be effective.

12.21   The Government is therefore committed to the faster processing of claims, dealing with the current impediments which restrict removal of those without authority to remain in the UK, and pursuing such alternatives to detention which enable the whereabouts of immigration offenders and failed asylum seekers to be known and removals to be effected.

Chapter 13

Implementation

13.1   This White Paper has set out a comprehensive and long-term strategy for modernising our immigration control. Implementing that strategy will involve a major programme of work, including:

- additional resources; and

- legislation.

13.2   Delivering the new strategy will present new challenges and opportunities for all immigration staff. The additional resources being provided at key points in the system will help to relieve the pressures which would otherwise have been bound to increase. New legislation, and streamlined and flexible procedures should enable future pressures to be better managed. Modernisation will help to provide the tools necessary to strengthen the control and improve the quality of service to the public. Consistent with those objectives, IND is committed to achieving Investors in People status by the year 2000.

Spending plans

13.3   Investment in immigration control and case handling is key to the strategy proposed in this White Paper. The Government intends to modernise the control and provide a better service to genuine travellers, while deterring abusive asylum seekers and others with no claim to be here. We shall also deal more quickly with all types of cases, but particularly asylum applications and appeals. Speedier disposal of asylum cases will reduce the cost of supporting asylum seekers and these savings will more than pay for the investment.

13.4   The IND spending limits will increase by £120 million over the three years from April 1999. The Lord Chancellor's Department plans to spend an extra £20 million on the Immigration Appellate Authority over the same period. In addition the entry clearance operation, run by the Foreign and Commonwealth Office, costs about £65 million annually. This cost is fully covered by visa and entry clearance fees and future spending on entry clearance will vary broadly in line with demand.

13.5   Early chapters of this Paper have indicated what the Government plans to achieve with the additional funds. The main points are:

- increased numbers of asylum decisions so that, on current forecasts of asylum claims, the backlog will be cleared and decision times of two months or less will be achieved by April 2001;

- expansion of the immigration appeals system, with the aim of reducing the average waiting time for an appeal to an adjudicator to four months by April 2001;

- increased removals of failed asylum seekers;

- expansion of the network of airline liaison officers to reduce the numbers of inadequately documented passengers travelling to the UK; and

- increasing the capacity to determine more citizenship applications in order to reduce backlogs and waiting times.

More detail is contained in the Annex.

13.6   The Government is also reforming the budgeting and planning arrangements.

Financial responsibility for asylum seeker support will transfer to the Home Office from April 1999. Home Office provision includes £900 million over the three year period to cover this expenditure. The new arrangements for supporting asylum seekers will be a direct Home Office responsibility. But until the new system is fully implemented the Home Office will transfer funds to meet the costs of benefits such as income support and housing benefit and of local authorities' support for asylum seekers under the National Assistance Act 1948 or the Children's Act 1989.

13.7   There will also be an integrated planning process involving all Government Departments which bear responsibility for immigration control activity, immigration appeals or for providing support or facilities for asylum seekers or people from abroad who do have a claim to be here. This will ensure that the system is managed more effectively, the processes are fair, fast and firm and the total cost to the taxpayer is kept as low as possible.

Charging

13.8   Much of the cost of the immigration control – and, therefore, the additional resources to modernise it – will need to be met from general taxation. But an ever-growing number of both individuals and business enterprises benefit from the growth in international travel and the Government thinks it right to explore whether a greater proportion of the costs of immigration control should be borne by those who are direct beneficiaries of the increase. These might include passengers, airlines, shipping companies and port authorities (ie seaport authorities, airport authorities and the CRTL authority).

13.9   At present there is power to charge applicants who apply for settlement status in the UK. But the Government will consider whether it would be right to broaden the scope of this power in order to charge for any application to remain in this country. This

would put applicants who apply to extend their stay from within the UK more on a par with those who decide to establish their immigration status before travelling to this country and who pay the appropriate fee for an entry certificate. This would be fairer for applicants as a whole.

13.10   The Government will also examine the arrangements for providing facilities for the immigration control. The Home Secretary has a statutory power to direct port authorities to make available facilities for the immigration control. But no enterprise which is as large as the Immigration Service and so important to the security of this country can operate without backup facilities which, in the very nature of things, have to be available on the spot. We will, therefore, in partnership with port authorities, consider whether there is a case for additional facilities to be provided at ports of entry.

13.11   For some years the Immigration Service has been empowered to provide additional immigration services to carriers and port authorities on payment of a charge. This has provided port authorities and carriers with a degree of choice in the level of service they wish to provide to their customer. Where the provision of such additional services serves to improve the efficiency and effectiveness of the on-entry control, the Government has no wish to restrict such opportunities. But we will consider clarifying the existing law with a view to making clear which immigration services will be provided against a charge.

Legislation

13.12   The following elements of the strategy can only be achieved with primary legislation:

Chapter 5

- right of appeal for those refused a visa to visit a family member; and

- financial bond scheme for visitors.

Chapter 6

- introduce greater operational flexibility.

Chapter 7

- possible statutory code of practice on checks to prevent illegal working;
- streamline the system of asylum and immigration appeals; and
- regulate unscrupulous immigration advisers.

Chapter 8

- rationalise the support arrangements to ensure that asylum seekers are not left destitute.

Chapter 9

- abolish the "White List".

Chapter 11

- strengthen existing criminal offences for obtaining leave to enter or remain by deception;
- additional powers for immigration officers; and
- extend the use of fingerprinting.

Chapter 12

- extend judicial element in the detention process;
- statutory rules on management and administration of detention centres; and
- specific powers for detention custody officers.

Chapter 13

- extend powers to charge for services; and
- extend reserve powers to require control facilities to be provided at ports.

13.13   The Government will introduce legislation as soon as possible to implement these elements of the strategy.

ANNEX

SPENDING PLANS

	Outturn 96/97	Outturn 97/98	Plans 98/99	Provisional Plans		
				99/00	00/01	01/02
IND Budget[1]	£207.7m	£203.2m	£208m	£237m	£252m	£259m
Passengers arriving	74m	80m	84m	88m	92m	97m
Asylum decisions	39,000	36,000	34,000	59,000	65,000	65,000
After Entry Decisions[2]	175,000	200,000	200,000	200,000	205,000	210,000
Removals of failed **Asylum Seekers**	4,800	7,100	6,000	8,000	10,000	12,000
Nationality Decisions[3]	43,700	54,500	44,500	84,000	91,000	91,000
Cost of Immigration **Appellate Authority** **(LCD)**	£11.4m	£12.5m	£13.3m	£18.9m	£24m	£17.7m
Appeals disposals[4]	29,000	35,400	39,000	46,000	60,000	45,000
Cost of Entry Clearance **Operation**	£60.2m	£62.5m	£65m	n/a	n/a	n/a
Visa/Entry Clearance **Applications**[5]	1.6m (1996)	1.5m (1997)	1.5m (1998)	1.6m (1999)	1.7m (2000)	n/a
Asylum Seekers Support **(Provisional)**	n/a	n/a	£350m	£350m	£300m	£250m

Notes:

(1) In order to give a comparable line of figures, adjustments have been made to reflect a classification change in receipts and the cost of a major building project, provision for which was originally transferred to the Home Office from the Property Holdings Agency.

(2) Applications for extensions of stay and for settlement.

(3) Projections for 1999/2000 and beyond assume that fee receipts can be applied to meet the direct costs of processing cases. The details of this have yet to be agreed.

(4) Asylum and non-asylum appeals.

(5) Figures are for calendar years as shown.

Printed in the UK for The Stationery Office Limited on behalf of the
Controller of Her Majesty's Stationery Office
Dd 5068208   7/98   65536   J0054222   29/43408